CREDIT AND COLLECTION

Letters Ready to Go!

ED HALLORAN

D1605421

NTC Business Books
NTC/Contemporary Publishing Company

Library of Congress Cataloging-in-Publication Data

Halloran, Edward Joseph.
    Credit and collection letters ready to go! / Ed Halloran.
       p.   cm.
    ISBN 0-8442-3569-5
    1. Collecting of accounts.   I. Title.
    HG3752.5.H35   1998
    658.8'8—dc21   97-42298
                                          CIP

To Maria Cristina,
who makes everything interesting
and the vast majority of things possible

Cover design by Nick Panos
Interior design by City Desktop Productions, Inc.

Published by NTC Business Books
An imprint of NTC/Contemporary Publishing Company
4255 West Touhy Avenue, Lincolnwood (Chicago), Illinois 60646-1975 U.S.A.
Copyright © 1998 by NTC/Contemporary Publishing Company
All rights reserved. No part of this book may be reproduced, stored in a retrieval system, or transmitted in any form or by any means, electronic, mechanical, photocopying, recording, or otherwise, without the prior permission of NTC/Contemporary Publishing Company.
Printed in the United States of America
International Standard Book Number: 0-8442-3569-5

15   14   13   12   11   10   9   8   7   6   5   4   3   2   1

Contents

Preface

Many people who become entrepreneurs or consultants come from relatively large corporations. Larger firms annually write off a certain percentage of their receivables as bad debt. Few people who aren't directly involved with credit and collections have any concept of how much bad debt a company can live with; they only know that uncollectable accounts are part of the cost of doing business.

While larger firms aren't thrilled when an account goes bad, they do have the resources to carry on. Unfortunately, small businesses and individuals trying to make a go of it are generally ill-prepared to handle past-due receivables and as a result go out of business at a rapid rate.

Those who survive and prosper have carefully thought through their credit and collection policies and taken steps to grant credit wisely and collect aggressively. Letters are an important part of their day-to-day business. The sample letters in this book are valuable only if you have done your homework! After all, if debtors were to read this book, and it consisted of nothing more than model letters, they would be able to determine how many letters they could ignore until you would become "serious."

Collection letters progress from friendly reminders to a notice that you are forwarding the past-due account to an agency or attorney. The letters, whether generated by the primary creditor or by an agency or attorney, possess both *timing* (e.g., 30 days, 60 days past due) and *tone* (becoming blunter as time goes on).

Frequently, though, collection letters lack the third "T," *tenacity*, which is what makes it clear to the debtor that you are on top of things, and you must be taken seriously.

In addition to teaching you when and what to write, this book will also teach you how to back up those letters with positive actions that will enable you to grant credit wisely and effect collections in a timely manner. In the process, your business will prosper.

Timing . . . Tone . . . Tenacity: These are the hallmarks of a true professional!

Acknowledgments

My thanks to John Beutelschies; Bob Hirsch; Larry Colley; Jim Rowe; Bill Corbett; Chuck Brock; Connie Romero; Bob Rundle; Joe Jackson; Bene Schafer; Herb Cohen; Rich Hagle; Rich Wilson; Cathy Linscott; Sandy Segrist; Teresa Donohue; Doretha Jones; Marilyn Bilyeu; Vera Whitworth; Ross Lowr; Brock Adjustment Co., Inc.; Jackson Sound Productions, Ltd.; and The National Association of Credit Management.

Part I

The Process of Credit

Chapter 1

Extending Credit: Where It All Begins

Years ago, a consumer lending officer at a large bank told me, "I have all of my lenders spend their first six months on the job working the phones in our collection department. I do this because I want them to know what can go wrong with people and businesses that once had good credit. That way, when it's time to begin making loans, our people will avoid making many of the mistakes made by overly enthusiastic lenders at other institutions."

He went on to stress that granting credit is never a risk-free proposition and, indeed, unless you are willing to take some chances, you will never make any money. The key is to be able to determine the people who are good risks and to handle their accounts in an intelligent, professional manner.

It begins with deciding how much credit you are willing to extend to an individual or business. In the preface, I mentioned that larger firms are able, however reluctantly, to write off some of their bad accounts. Small companies and consultants, though, are seldom in a position to go very long without getting paid in full by all of their customers (and in some cases, they may only have one!).

Your ability to grant credit depends upon your resources. No matter how good a firm's or individual's bona fides are, you should be in a position to cover your losses if your client suddenly goes belly-up. After all, if you don't get paid and you were relying on receivables to pay yourself and your creditors, you're a prime candidate for going belly-up yourself!

Most small ventures fail because of a lack of working capital, and unfortunately a lot of consultants who get stiffed also go under. Those who succeed do so because they took the time to check references and granted an affordable amount of credit (i.e., only as much money as they could afford to write off completely).

Joe Jackson, whose credit application we'll look at later in this book, is a very successful businessman. From the beginning, he was careful about extending credit. Joe says, "Individuals and other businesses have to realize that you're in business, too. Asking for references up front and then checking them out is a prudent precaution that any good businessperson will take. Anyone who is unable or reluctant to provide references probably isn't worth dealing with!"

Potential clients or customers shouldn't be surprised or offended by your request that they fill out an application for credit that will include banking and other references. If they balk, you should walk.

You need to learn as much as possible about the people and businesses to whom you are going to grant credit, and you shouldn't extend credit until they have provided everything you have asked for.

Individuals should provide a financial statement, credit bureau report, tax returns, and banking and personal references. Let's talk about each of these.

Financial Statement

This should list their assets (e.g., bank accounts and real property) and their liabilities (e.g., credit card and mortgage balances). The end result will provide you with their net worth.

I once turned down an applicant whose net worth showed a negative balance. When he called to complain, he said to me, "Of course it's negative! I'm trying to avoid paying more taxes, but I'm really very well off!" He added, "Don't you know how the real world works?"

I mentioned to him that his tax returns for the past two years showed that he had a negative income, too. He replied, "See? That's how it's done!" I replied that if we ever ended up in court, I would look a bit foolish for granting credit to someone with a negative net worth and tax returns showing negative income. After cursing me, he said, "You just don't understand how business is conducted!"

Actually, I do, and I know that if you do not take certain risks, you will never get ahead. The key is to take affordable risks and, in this case, what he was asking for wasn't something that I could afford to give him.

Tax Returns

It is not prying to ask for copies of tax returns for the past two or three years. This enables you to determine if the person is being truthful when stating his or her income (at least through the most recent tax years).

Credit Bureau Report

By paying a fee, an individual is able to procure a narrative-style copy of his or her report. This is actually easier for someone with no credit background to read than a standard report, which can be rather complex.

Someone who refuses to provide a report should not receive credit. If an individual says, "I always pay cash," you can reply, "Fine! I accept cash." A report showing that a person has seldom or never availed himself of credit is not a negative thing, and his bona fides can be determined in other ways. However sketchy the report is, an individual should be willing to provide it to you.

It's also worth noting that, while bad credit tends to get reported, the good news isn't always there. That's why you need to ask for other forms of information.

You should also keep in mind the difference between secured and unsecured credit.

- *Secured credit:* The best examples of secured credit are houses and cars. Yes, mortgages and car payments are forms of big ticket credit, but, if someone goes into default, she can lose her home and/or transportation, so she is least likely to get behind on these loans. As a result, payment history in these areas is likely to be good.

- *Unsecured credit:* Here's where you can find out how a person handles money. Revolving charge cards indicate how responsible people are (as opposed to travel and entertainment cards, e.g., American Express, where the full balance must be paid monthly). After all, once he avails himself of the funds, there is nothing to secure the debt other than his promise to pay.

It's actually possible for a person to have too much credit available. Some people will proudly say, "Look at how many banks and companies are willing to lend money to me, and I don't even use it all." Your job is to compute exactly how deeply into debt an individual could go if he actually did avail himself of everything that has been offered to him. Many of us who have large amounts of potential credit would not be able to pay our bills if we used all (or even most) of it. In fact, a lot of our financial lives are based on at least two incomes, and, if one job is lost, the house of cards will collapse.

It's important to remember that it takes weeks, in some cases months, for new balances to make it onto a credit bureau report. An applicant may have already fully tapped other resources prior to coming to you. That's why it's important to get a full disclosure from everyone to whom you are extending credit. Later, if the loan goes sour, you may be able to allege (and substantiate) fraud if they provided you with false information at the outset. (This will be discussed in more detail later.)

Credit bureaus allow individuals to provide brief explanations for periods of slow payment. An example from my own life came when, in a two-month period, I was laid off, my wife died after a long illness, and I took a new job that paid less than my previous one. I worked with my mortgage company and other creditors and finally got back on an even keel, and my partial payments were not held against me.

Illness, accidents, death, layoffs, and divorce happen, and people who are willing to work with their creditors are usually able to turn things around. Don't be put off by someone who had a bad patch in her life for valid reasons, provided she got things squared away in a responsible manner.

Banking References

A person or firm should provide you with information concerning their bank(s). This book provides a form and a letter for checking bank references. Take the time to use them!

When you receive your first check from a client or customer, copy it. That way, you'll have a record of where he banks, which is always useful if you have to garnishee at some point. The check will provide you with the name, location, and phone number of the bank; the account number; and the month and year when the account was opened.

Each time you receive a payment, see if there are any changes before you deposit the check. Then, if your customer changes banks, you can make a copy of the check from his new bank and have that information. Do not throw out the copy of the check from the previous bank, as your customer may still be doing business with that bank. (More on this later.)

Personal References

At first glance, this would seem to be a no-brainer. After all, anyone on this list would be expected to provide a glowing reference, so why check? There are two reasons. First, it is a way of finding out if the people who are listed know the applicant well enough (or at all) to be able to provide a reference. More than one scoundrel has listed impressive names in order to intimidate the credit grantor, figuring that no calls will be made. Check it out!

The other reason for calling is that if everything is on the up-and-up, the people who were listed as references are likely to let the applicant know that you check things out, indicating that you take business relationships seriously.

Timing, Tone, and Tenacity: The Keys to Successful Collection Letters

Timing

Ironically, your first collection letter is the one that welcomes a new client or customer. It sets the scene for your delivery of valuable goods or services. Your product must have what marketing people term "utility," which means that you are providing something of value in return for something of value to you (money).

Provided that you keep your word in terms of meeting your deadlines and providing a quality product, you have every right (including legal) to expect that your customer or client will keep his or her end of the bargain and pay you in full and on time.

If you take a professional approach regarding payment terms from the outset, things are more likely to run smoothly. So, when payments are late, phone calls and letters are perfectly in order. Initially, you're friendly and firm. Keep in mind that, even if the debtor is a "little bit" late, he or she is, in essence, borrowing money from you, usually interest-free. That's why it's important to take action right away.

Tone

Your tone should always be professional and so should your words. As time goes along, if you are still not getting paid, the friendliness in your voice will disappear. That's understandable, but keep your words within the boundaries of good taste and the law. Don't threaten people, and don't use abusive language, even if they do. Instead remind them of the original agreement, your compliance with the terms, and your expectations concerning their responsibilities.

If you realize that you're not getting anywhere, it's time to make a decision concerning your next course of action. When you decide to pass the debt along to an agency or an attorney, inform the debtor, and then do it! (In fact, you are legally obligated to do so.)

Small-claims court may also be an option, although I believe that a good agency or an attorney are better alternatives. We will look at all of your options in subsequent chapters.

Tenacity

Collection activities tend to be unpleasant, and inexperienced creditors are prone to vacillation. Delaying plays right into the debtor's hands and avails you nothing.

This book provides you with a structured approach to effecting collections. If you follow the prescribed actions when you decide which avenue to pursue, your course will be clear and all you will have to do is be tenacious about following through.

A real pro in any area of endeavor is always businesslike in his or her approach to problems, and simply does the work in a thorough and timely manner.

Timing, Tone, Tenacity: These are the hallmarks of a professional person, and you should make them your own!

Chapter 2

Using Investigators, Agencies, and Attorneys

Debt does not improve with age. When you conclude that you are unable to effect collections on your own, it's time to take another course of action.

The first step is to admit to yourself that there is a possibility that you may never collect a cent on the bad account. It is imperative that you have enough money to cover your losses and keep your business going in the event that a given client or customer fails to pay you. Not getting paid is the worst-case scenario, and it behooves you to face that contingency up front. Once you do that, you are ready to attempt to salvage something from the wreckage.

As a collections pro once told me, "You can't lose the money twice!" Simply put, if you write off a bad debt as uncollectable, anything that you are subsequently able to recover goes directly to your bottom line.

During the savings and loan scandals of the 1980s, many financial institutions carried uncollectable balances in their assets columns, implying that those debts would eventually be paid in full. For a brief period this practice enabled them to "improve" their bottom lines, but reality eventually caught up with them.

When you realize that you cannot collect, it's time to charge off the account in full and pass it along to someone else, hoping that they will be able to recover at least a portion of it for you. Doing this enables you to get on with more productive work, including drumming up new business.

Generally speaking, the courses of action open to creditors when they charge off a bad debt are as follows:

1. Forget about it. This is only acceptable if you believe the balance due is too small to bother with.

2. Conduct an asset search yourself, or hire an investigator to do it for you. In any event, this should be done prior to opting for either of the next three alternatives.

3. Place it with an agency.

4. Turn it over to an attorney.

5. Take it to small-claims court (discussed in Chapter 3).

The Asset Search

The credit information we discussed in the first chapter comes in handy here. It's time to take apart the financial statement again, check for bank accounts, perform drive-by inspections, and so on. You can either do this on your own or pay someone else to do it for you.

Investigators

Investigators are only too happy to do things for you that, in many cases, you can do on your own for a lot less money. An investigator is likely to quote a lower hourly rate for asset searching that an attorney will. The ironic thing is that if you allow a law firm to conduct an investigation for you, you may be billed at the attorney's hourly rate (or very close to it), even though he or she likely will hire a low-cost investigator to do the work.

You are the best person to conduct a prelegal or pre-agency asset search because if you performed a thorough credit check at the outset, you can quickly determine what assets the debtor still has. Most of what investigators will provide you is readily available public information—in other words, information you can just as easily get for yourself, if you have the time to do so. The forms and checklists in Parts II and III will enable you to get the job done.

Agencies

Agencies come in all sizes. However, large agencies are better able to set up tape-to-tape transfers with their clients and are well-situated for dealing with large-volume operations, such as banks, hospitals, and mortgage companies. They tend to have computerized systems that bring up files on their collectors' screens. Everything is very efficient.

It's becoming more and more difficult for debtors to hide. Thanks to highly personalized account files and computer chips embedded in charge, debit, and credit cards, skip-tracing (locating someone who has left town) is not as difficult as it was just a few years ago. However, certain states remain debtors' havens due to their collection laws (Florida and Texas come readily to mind), so merely finding someone isn't a guarantee that payment will be forthcoming. Besides, no matter where a debtor is living, it's still possible to conceal funds in offshore accounts.

The average agency "creams" accounts; it tends to work the easy ones. If its initial letter and phone call have failed to yield promising results, the agency begins to lose interest and devotes the bulk of its time to mining more productive veins.

The problem from your standpoint is that the debt is important to you, and you are under the impression that it is being pursued aggressively. Meanwhile, the agency is not likely to say anything to you until they decide that you should "go legal," or sue.

Many agencies do not send staff members out to call on debtors personally because of the cost involved in putting people in the field. Most tend to rely on letters and phone calls, just as you did.

Placing a business debt with an agency escalates collection activities somewhat, but it's no guarantee that a debtor will pay up. The biggest single advantage is that the matter is out of your hands, and you are free to work on more important things.

It's not helpful to know what an agency's rate of collection is, because every debt is different. The only rate that matters is what percentage the agency will take when and if it actually collects something. It is helpful to the agency (and an attorney) if you have a bottom line figure in mind when negotiating a settlement. Yes, it's depressing to think about a debtor getting away with *anything* but settlements are frequently the only way that at least some money can be recovered.

Agencies (and attorneys) will naturally want to collect as much as possible, because they are being paid on a contingency fee basis, which means they receive a percentage of what they collect. They also have an inclination to work out settlements, so that they can guarantee making something acceptable on the deal.

All of this doesn't thrill you, I'm sure, but effecting collections takes time, which means that it costs money to make the effort. One way or another, it is going to cost you money, and good agencies are worthy of their hire, as are good attorneys. Since you have already physically and emotionally written off the past-due balance on the books, anything that comes your way is found money. It's only fair that you split the proceeds with the person(s) who helped you find it!

Attorneys

Attorneys can help you get the job done in one of two ways: They will effect collections, or the debtor will end up in bankruptcy court. Either way, the situation is resolved.

I recommend skipping the agency step where large balances are concerned. This way your attorney will receive a "fresher" debt, meaning that the likelihood of collecting is greater.

A good way to begin is with a letter from the attorney. You will pay a flat fee for this, but it may be enough to do the job. Briefly, the attorney states that she has consulted with you and believes the debt to be collectable. She urges the debtor to contact you by a certain date to make payment arrangements, indicating that this would be a wise course of action because any further delay on the debtor's part could cause him to incur additional costs. If the letter works, you are on your way. If not, it is time to sue.

We will discuss the small-claims court option (my least favorite) in the next chapter. Let's deal with "going legal" by using a lawyer.

First, find yourself an attorney who is well-acquainted with effecting collections. He or she will take the case on a contingency fee basis, but you will have some out-of-pocket expenses at the outset, such as process serving and filing fees. After that, the attorney's meter stops running, unless you agree to pay for an asset search.

Happily, if you conduct your own investigation, you will not have to pay the attorney (or anyone else) a dime. All you will need to do is provide your lawyer with the information you uncover.

Once the account is placed with an attorney, there is nothing further for you to do. You are free to get on with your life, knowing that you have done everything possible to collect the money owed to you. The attorney will see to it that the debtor is served and go about getting a court date.

Your lawyer can also negotiate your bottom-line settlement figure. During the pretrial period, you may hear from the debtor. All you need to do is refer him or her to your attorney, as the matter is now out of your hands. I heartily recommend this course of action, because it lets you get on with other work.

If you do hear from the debtor, don't be surprised to receive a variation on one of the following themes:

1. "Can't we work something out?" Your reply should be, "My attorney is handling this for me. Do you need the number?"

2. "If you push this, I'll take bankruptcy!" Your reply should be, "Petitioning the court for relief through bankruptcy is an option. The trial date is set, and everything is being handled by my attorney. Do you need the number?"

3. "Listen, I know I shouldn't be talking about this while the court case is pending, but I'm in a position to throw some more business your way if we can work things out." Your reply should be, "You're right, you shouldn't be talking to me about this at this time. My attorney is handling the court case. Do you need the number?"

A court date not only tells the debtor you are serious, but it also affords him some breathing room, as all other collection activities must cease once you "go legal"—unless, of course, the debtor (or his lawyer) has contacted your attorney and begun to negotiate.

Sometimes, negotiations take place, literally, on the courthouse steps. Or, once both parties are before a judge, he or she may send them into a conference room to see if something can be worked out.

A negotiated settlement will include the debtor's stipulation that, in effect, the settlement is a judgment, and if the debtor fails to live up to the terms of the agreement the debt reverts to the full amount due and the creditor is free to garnishee.

If the debtor fails to appear (or send an attorney), you will receive a default judgment, and then it is up to you to collect. Generally speaking, I suggest that you have your attorney handle having writs of garnishment served, rather than doing it yourself.

A judgment does not mean that you will get your money, but it provides you with an excellent opportunity for making the attempt, as you are now in a legal position to garnishee wages (if applicable), perform till-taps, or receive money from the debtor's bank accounts.

Serving Summons

Investigators will serve a summons for you, usually on a flat-fee basis, although if you're not in a hurry, law officers will also effect service for a fee. Generally, they will serve the summons within a week or so of their department's receiving it (along with the fee).

If possible, I suggest having a law officer do it, as it lends weight to the proceeding. If the debtor, through her attorney, says that she never received the summons, it is nice to be able to point out that it was served by a local law enforcement officer rather than a hired hand.

Process servers don't go to court unless they are summoned. A number of years ago, our agency pursued a high-roller deadbeat (for a client who hired us as investigators, rather than as collectors). I skip-traced him and effected service personally.

He was operating in an upscale office suite and had a waiting room filled with clients. I discreetly gave the receptionist my card and asked if I could see her boss for a moment. She went into his private office and emerged a short time later and ushered me in. I verified his identity and told him that I had not wanted to embarrass him in front of his clients by causing a scene. He said, "I appreciate that very much," and accepted the summons.

Months later, on his court date, I accompanied our client's attorney to the courthouse. I stayed out of sight until the debtor's attorney alleged that the debtor had never been properly served. Our client's attorney said, "Your honor, the man who effected service is present today and is willing to testify under oath." At that point, I came forward, and the deadbeat whispered something to his lawyer, who promptly withdrew his earlier statement and got on with the proceedings.

If a law officer had served the summons, the deadbeat probably would not have attempted to deny having been served. He banked on the fact that most civilian process servers do not show up at the trial. When a little extra time doesn't matter, I suggest that you always employ a law enforcement agency to serve the summons. That way, you have a worthwhile (in print) statement that it has been done.

Process servers, investigators, and repossession specialists can be found in the Yellow Pages. I advocate letting third parties do the legwork when it comes to the more unpleasant tasks. That way the situation is less likely to escalate than it would if you were to confront the debtor personally.

Timing

The moment you determine that you cannot collect on your own, decide whether you are going to place the account with an agency or use an attorney. When you do this, take action. Notify the debtor, conduct an asset search, and turn the account over to a pro.

Tone

Be professional in your letter and on the phone (should the debtor call). You have made a business decision, and the matter is now in other hands.

Tenacity

Now that you have charged off the balance and the account is no longer in-house, let it go! It's time to devote your efforts to your core business and give yourself wholeheartedly to working for people who pay!

Chapter 3

Small-Claims Court and Bankruptcies

As I mentioned earlier, small-claims court is my least favorite option. This might strike you as strange, because I suggest performing prelegal investigations on your own to save money, rather than hiring an investigator directly or through an attorney.

Having said that, I suggest passing the investigation file along to an attorney, paying the service and filing fees, and then splitting the proceeds, if any, with your lawyer. It's fair to ask, "How will that save me money?" Well, go back a few words to "if any." The fact is you may never recover a cent. However, bringing an attorney on board escalates the matter from the debtor's point of view and greatly increases your chances of getting paid.

After all, the case will not be heard in small-claims court, where you would have to do all of the work because attorneys are not allowed. Now lawyers are involved, and in order to be properly represented, the debtor will have to do something he or she hates: pay—for an attorney of his or her own.

True, the only person who is assured of getting paid is the debtor's lawyer, but the fact that you are willing to go to the extent of engaging an attorney of your own indicates that this is no small matter to you. Taking this step is more likely to work than if you were to go through the small-claims court process.

Small-Claims Court

If you opt to take this course of action, you will have to pay someone to effect service, as you are not allowed to do it yourself. The clerk at the small-claims court will tell you just what you will need to do.

Have a law officer serve the summons. He or she is likely to be in uniform when they go to the debtor's home or place of business to effect service, and it will make quite an impression.

Going through a small-claims court is a lot of work. I suggest attending a session to learn the drill prior to your own appearance.

When months later your day in court comes, you will be representing yourself, so you will need to have everything ready to make your case. Getting ready puts a lot of pressure on you, because there is always a chance that you will lose, so you are likely to do a fair amount of worrying. I would rather pass that burden on to an attorney, because where small-claims court is concerned, many deadbeats simply do not show up! Meanwhile, you have been worrying about things the entire time.

If the other party doesn't show and you do, after you state your case, the judge awards you a default judgment. You've won! The fact is, you still have a debt to collect, and you will either have to do that on your own or hire someone else to do it for you. Meanwhile, the debtor continues to skate.

If there is any potential for a situation escalating into violence, I urge you to hire a professional to perform till-taps, repossessions, and wage and salary garnishments for you. Generally speaking, garnisheeing bank accounts is something you can do yourself, once you obtain a judgment and procure and complete a proper writ of garnishment. The legal forms you will need vary from state to state. Begin by asking the clerk at small-claims court if it issues forms; if it doesn't, the clerk will be able to tell you who publishes them in your state and where you will be able to procure them.

A consultant who had been stiffed by a firm that also owed a large sum of money to my company took the small-claims route. He collected 100¢ on the dollar, largely because, having already used an attorney to collect the money due to my firm, I had no qualms about telling the consultant about the bank accounts I had uncovered during my prelegal investigation. Otherwise, he might still be hunting!

Referring the debtor to your attorney helps you retain emotional stability and increases the likelihood that, if nothing else, a settlement can be worked out. In my opinion, in most cases small-claims court is a mug's game!

Bankruptcies

Years ago if someone were on the verge of declaring bankruptcy he would at least have the decency to leave town. Nowadays, bankruptcies have virtually no stigma, thanks to large corporations that have managed to turn things around by stiffing earlier creditors and paying new ones.

First, let me say a word in defense of the bankruptcy laws. They are designed to help people and organizations who, for perfectly legitimate reasons, can't pay their bills. The laws are there for good reason.

"I'm going to take bankruptcy!" is something that many a debtor has said through the years. In fact, a person or firm doesn't "take" bankruptcy; they petition the court for relief, and it won't be granted until any and all creditors have an opportunity to speak at the hearing.

Too often, though, particularly with large companies, once a debtor says, "Call my lawyer!" collection activities cease. The collector, having ascertained that the debtor has engaged an attorney and has received a filing number, will note which chapter the case falls under, enter the case number in the debtor's file, and, unless it's a large balance, that's it. As far as the creditor is concerned, the debtor is bankrupt, and the balance is written off. The creditor may not be inclined to send a representative to the hearing, which could be a big mistake as I will illustrate.

In 1996, the United States passed a dubious milestone when more than a million bankruptcies were awarded. This means that on more than a million occasions, creditors received little (Chapter 13) or nothing (Chapter 7). (Ask your attorney to explain to you about Chapter 11 bankruptcies and payment precedence in Chapter 13 cases.)

Bankruptcy attorneys advertise regularly in broadcast and print media. We've become inured to the idea of corporations and individuals filing bankruptcy, so we don't give it much thought as a general rule. We should though, even if we are not creditors, because people who have abused credit cause us to pay higher interest rates and prices.

And, if we are creditors, we should be very interested in what goes on at bankruptcy court, particularly when a person or firm that owes us money is seeking relief. It may well behoove you to ascertain the day of the hearing and, when the time rolls around, go yourself or hire someone to represent you.

The first thing you will learn by going to the hearing is whether the debtor shows up (a rather surprising number of people do not). That might strike you as ridiculous. She paid an attorney to file for her, so why would she waste the money?

Well, a true deadbeat would not consider it wasted. Many creditors, after hearing the magic word, "bankruptcy" followed by the chapter and filing numbers, simply give up. A few keystrokes from the collector will award the designation "bankrupt" to the debtor, even though no one has had their day in court.

Think about it; if you owed many creditors large sums of money and could get rid of their calls and letters simply by engaging an attorney to file for you (for a rather small fee), wouldn't you consider doing it? And, if you knew that your creditors thought the bankruptcy was a done deal, and they probably would not find out that you hadn't actually gone through with it, wouldn't the temptation to forget the whole thing be rather strong? More than a few hardcore deadbeats have pulled this scam; don't let them victimize you!

Not going through with the actual proceedings enables the debtor later to truthfully answer "no" to the common credit application question, "Have you ever been adjudged a bankrupt?" Meanwhile, the debtor avoids paying past creditors anything.

Let's say that, like most people, a debtor does show up for the hearing. Further, let's also say that, as in most cases, the whole thing is legitimate, and the trustee approves his payment plan for a Chapter 13 or writes off everything with a Chapter 7. OK, it's resolved, and you know that for certain.

But there is another scenario, one that unfolds when someone has lied on a credit application by not disclosing existing debts that would have disqualified him from having additional credit extended to him. When this happens, certain creditors are able to allege fraud and possibly have their balances excluded from discharge. Let me give you a real-life example.

When I was still in banking, one of our collectors smelled a rat when a fellow who owed us $7,500 (plus interest) said that he was nearly $1 million in debt and planning to file for bankruptcy. The amount he cited did not square with the information he had provided to us when he applied for his credit line. Armed with a copy of his original application and his credit file, I went to the hearing.

When I arrived, I saw a friend who worked for another bank. It turned out that our debtor had hit them for a little over $15,000, and that they also were wondering where the "nearly $1 million" in additional debt had come from. When the trustee asked if any creditors were present, we identified ourselves and were allowed to speak.

We said that had we known about the additional debts (which were not listed on the original applications and did not appear on his credit bureau report), we would never have extended credit. Since those debts were already owed prior to the filing of the application and he had not revealed them to us, we alleged fraud. The trustee called for a brief recess, during which the debtor's attorney agreed to exclude our accounts from the bankruptcy. When the hearing resumed, the trustee accepted the set asides and asked if any additional creditors were present. None of them were, which is unfortunate because the dates of many of those debts were after we had extended credit, meaning that fraud could also have been alleged by those creditors. By not being present, they waived their opportunity to be heard, and their balances were erased along with the others when the Chapter 7 was awarded.

Meanwhile, we were paid as was the other bank. After having gotten rid of hundreds of thousands of dollars in indebtedness, the debtor was able to pay us off in full.

In this case, our *timing* (the hearing date), *tone* (firm and professional), and *tenacity* (our follow through) carried the day. However, most of the time when a bankruptcy is over with, you will have little or nothing to show for it. That is why it is so important to grant credit wisely and work past-due accounts early on, thereby minimizing your chances for losing money down the road.

How Bad Can It Get?

Here are some actual figures for recent business bankruptcies (obviously from the size of their liabilities, they were once considered excellent credit risks):

Liabilities	Assets
$265,730	$100
$75,312	$2,992
$140,539	$3,749
$87,359	$1,491

And last, one of my all-time favorites, a diversified little group of businesses that managed to amass $2,028,554 in debts, which were "covered" by a whopping $4,331 in assets. In every instance, one or more firms or individuals had extended credit to these businesses and, as each bankruptcy was a Chapter 7, their creditors had to write off 100¢ on the dollar.

It's not a pretty picture, and you will derive cold comfort from being a creditor when little or nothing is forthcoming after the bankruptcy is awarded. That's why it is so important to check thoroughly at the beginning of a business relationship.

Hardcore deadbeats are predators, and like their counterparts in the wild, they tend to go after easy prey. Consultants and small business owners who, in their eagerness to begin or continue a business relationship, throw prudence to the wind, leave themselves wide open to the con artists of the world. Don't fall into this trap! If a prospective client or customer has a bad track record, insist upon cash in advance. And, if an existing client or customer starts slow-paying or not paying at all, cut off credit, pronto!

Timing

Begin with a detailed background check before you extend credit. The forms and letters in Parts II and III will serve you well. Should things go badly down the road, be ready to move promptly.

Tone

Be professional throughout the collections process. The old saying, "I don't get mad, I get even" applies here. Career deadbeats seem to delight in upsetting their creditors. Do not give them that satisfaction. Simply go about your business in a quiet, professional manner.

Tenacity

Although pushing things to resolution through either small-claims or bankruptcy court is not pleasant, real pros stick with the task. Consultants and companies with a reputation for not being lazy when it comes to bad debt tend to encounter fewer collection problems through the years. Believe me, the word gets around!

Chapter 4

Going Global: Overseas Collections

"Overseas" may be overstating the case because, thanks to NAFTA, you are as likely to be attempting to effect collections in Canada or Mexico as you are in some far-off land. In any event, dealing with another nation always complicates matters.

Several factors, which will be discussed in greater detail later, are simply part of the risk of doing business internationally. For example, currency fluctuations are difficult if not impossible to predict but can greatly affect the value of the money owed. Similarly, the differences and delays in the mail add to the difficulty of corresponding even with willing and honest creditors. When there is a problem, these obstacles only make the situation more difficult to resolve. In addition, there is the question of jurisdiction—whose courts are going to decide a legal matter?

In addition to all of these areas for serious trouble, there are cultural and linguistic barriers. Some cultures have a more "malleable" view of time—and when it is your money not theirs, it's unlikely that they will change without some gentle encouragement. Aside from other cultural differences, there is the problem of communication. In the words of an old Italian saying, *Traduttore, traditore* ("translator, traitor"): while you might be able to handle virtually all of the procedures in this book, translation is not an area for do-it-yourselfers—even if you are reasonably proficient in the language of the country where you are doing business. This is certainly one place to use a professional. Practical examples that address these issues are included later in this book.

As always, the first steps are most important. And in the case of foreign credit, it's imperative that you get things right the first time during the credit granting stage.

For example, if you are going to provide consulting services to a foreign entity, cover yourself by doing things on a retainer basis. Be sure to build enough money into your fee payments to make an acceptable profit for your time and effort.

If you are going to contract for goods and services to help you do the work for your foreign client, there are two ways to go:

1. Arrange for the client to gain credit from the various vendors whom you will employ and then simply administer things for the client. You should strive to arrange for a Hold Harmless Agreement for yourself (in writing) with the vendors, so that you are not liable in the event that the foreign client defaults. This will protect you financially, but don't be surprised if you lose a friend or two among the vendors should things turn sour.

2. An alternative is to make arrangements with the client to pay you enough to cover all expected expenses with U.S. vendors. This would be money above and beyond what you are paid for your services. There should also be a written proviso that if payments are delayed, work will be delayed, as it needs to be done on a pay-as-you-go basis.

In either case, it's not a good idea to make yourself liable for someone else's debts, because if something goes wrong with the primary debtor, his creditors will come after you. As an attorney who specializes in international trade issues said to me, "U.S. distributors for foreign manufacturers often find themselves functioning as no-charge 'banks,' rather than profit-making entities."

This phenomenon is not at all uncommon in the international sector. While the rewards are potentially great, and well worth pursuing, the risks are enormous, too, and not just for small businesses. Consultants are also at risk, and if you fall into this category, your best bet is to establish your billing policies along the lines discussed at the beginning of this chapter. If you suddenly have to cut off credit to a foreign client, you'll lose at most a month or two of income from her, but you will still be in business.

Foreign collections can be a dicey proposition. You might do better by selling the debt (if you can) to an agency or a syndicate that is willing to pay you cents on the dollar, rather than trying to fight it out overseas. We will delve into this further in Part II.

If this chapter has scared you off, good! You are too faint-hearted to do business globally. If it hasn't frightened you, apply the techniques discussed in this book, and you have a shot at making a go of it.

Business is never a risk-free proposition, and you have to be ready, emotionally and financially, to deal with setbacks in the marketplace. Government agencies, vendors, personnel, and consultants are not really your partners. In fact, you are working for them! Your job is to keep paying them in a timely manner. After you do so, hopefully there is a little something left over for you. Even if there isn't, the meters keep right on running. This is particularly true in the international sector, because almost everything takes longer when you "go global."

Part II

Sample Letters and Analysis

You will need the following forms to extend credit and effect collections. If you are a consultant or you run a small business, you cannot afford to tarry when it comes to collecting money. The more you string out the letter-writing process, the longer deadbeats have to string you along.

Step one is to cut off anyone who is stiffing you. It's easier to do this if your initial terms and conditions for extending credit spell things out clearly. Joe Jackson's credit application is a good starting point for you as you determine how you will conduct your business. While Chico and Groucho Marx had a great time tearing clauses out of a contract in one of their movies, Mr. Jackson's contract includes everything he needs to protect himself. (I caution you against acting like the Marx brothers, because getting your money is serious business.)

After you draft your application, terms, and conditions have them reviewed thoroughly by your attorney. The fee is money well spent, because you will protect yourself by doing things right the first time.

The letters and past due notices in Part II will need to be re-created on your own letterhead. The forms, however, are ready for copying.

Too often people who have become overextended by letting debtors slide don't want to face the grim news. They keep allowing deadbeats to tell them lies, hoping that somehow everything will turn out OK in the end.

Many will even go so far as to extend more credit to deadbeats, to stay on their good side. Consultants and small business with only one or two major clients or customers are particularly susceptible to this, as they are boxed in with nowhere to go. The deadbeats are well aware of this and continue to milk them.

I suggest that you move quickly and put the bad debts behind you, so that you can get on with more productive work. This means taking the agency or attorney route much more rapidly than a large company normally would. A large company tends to be slower because it has the financial resources to do so, and because of its size, it's less emotional about slow-pays and even no-pays. Simply put, you can't afford to operate this way.

Credit Application/Terms and Conditions of Sale

Many thanks to Joe Jackson of Jackson Sound Productions, Ltd., for providing a copy of his standard credit application. While this form isn't for everyone, you should find it easy to alter to meet your needs. Once you see what's on it, we will hit the highlights to show you how, in addition to being a superb form for determining how much (if any) credit you are willing to extend, it is also a great collections tool if things turn sour.

Firm name:_____ Contact person: _____

Address: _____

City:_____ State:_____ ZIP: _____

Kind of business: _____ In business since:_____

Telephone: _____ Resale number: _____

State sales tax resale #:_____ (Attach copy) Federal I.D.: _____

Purchase order required? Yes:_____ No: _____

Corporation: _____ Partnership: _____ Sole owner: _____

Principals: President: _____

              Vice pres.: _____

              Secretary: _____

Bank Reference

Name: _____ Acct. #:_____

Address: _____

City:_____ State:_____ ZIP: _____

Telephone: _____

Contact:_____ Banked here since: _____

Trade References

Firm name:_____ Telephone: _____

Address: _____

Contact: _____

Firm name:_____ Telephone: _____

Address: _____

Contact: _____

Firm name:_____ Telephone: _____

Address: _____

Contact: _____

The undersigned hereby agrees that should a credit account be opened, and in the event of default in the payment of any amount due, and if such account is submitted to a collection authority, to pay an additional charge equal to the cost of collection including court costs.

Applicant company _____ Date _____

Signature _____ Title _____

Full name of signator (please print) _____

1. Terms and Payment

(a) Terms of payment are 50% deposit with order, with balance due at time of delivery. Arrangements for credit must be made in advance. Purchaser agrees to submit its most current financial information and bank and trade references, if requested.

(b) All sales, use excise, or similar tax applicable to sales pursuant to this agreement shall be paid by the purchaser, unless purchaser provides seller with a Tax Exemption Certificate acceptable to the taxing authorities.

(c) In the event that the purchase account becomes overdue or delinquent, seller shall be entitled to reimbursement from purchaser for seller's reasonable expenses of collection, including attorney fees. Seller may charge the lesser of 1.5% per month or the highest lawful monthly contract rate on overdue accounts.

2. Price, Shipment, and Delivery Terms

(a) Due to the uncertainty of costs, prices are subject to change without notice.

(b) All deliveries are F.O.B. seller's facility.

3. Warranty: Limitation of Liability

(a) Seller warrants to the original purchaser that the product will be free from defects in material and workmanship for a period of 30 days from date of delivery. Seller's sole liability (and purchaser's only remedy) for any defect shall be to replace or repair, at seller's option, any materials which seller reasonably determines to have a defect covered by its warranty within a reasonable time, and without charge.

(b) Except for the repair/replacement described in this paragraph, seller shall not be liable for damages of any kind arising out of either the use of the material furnished hereunder or its failure to function properly.

(c) Material which has been subject to alteration, misuse, misapplication, negligence or action shall be excluded from warranty coverage.

The above warranty is in lieu of any other warranty, whether express, implied, or statutory including but not limited to any warranty of merchantability fitness for any particular purpose, freedom from infringement, or the like, and any warranty otherwise arising out of any proposal, specification, or sample. Seller neither assumes nor authorizes any person to assume for it any other liability.

4. Exclusion of Damages

In no event shall seller be liable for any consequential, incidental, indirect, exemplary, or special damages, whether in contract or in tort, in any action, in connection with this agreement or the material furnished hereunder.

5. Rights, Licenses, Copyrights, and Indemnification

(a) Purchaser shall secure all rights, licenses, and copyrights for anything to be recorded, produced, or duplicated in any way by seller. Purchaser warrants that it is the legal owner or licensee for purposes of duplication for any material supplied to seller, and seller shall be held harmless by purchaser from any and all claims by third parties.

(b) Purchaser shall indemnify and hold seller harmless from all suits, claims, demands, and other clauses of action and expenses arising out of or in connection with the production, duplication, or distribution of products, materials, or services that seller shall have furnished.

6. General

(a) The interpretation and performance of this agreement are governed by the laws of the State of _____.

(b) It is agreed that sales are made on the terms, conditions, and warranties contained herein. To the extent of any conflict, these terms and conditions take precedence over any on purchaser's order form. No agreement shall be valid unless in writing, duly signed by the parties.

7. Merchandise Return

Seller must be notified within 30 days from the date of delivery or pickup or purchaser's order of any problem, defect, miscount, or other reason for the return of any merchandise ordered.

8. Customer Property

(Seller's corporate name) is not responsible for any loss or damage of/to materials or master tapes stored or used. (Seller's corporate name)'s insurance does not cover this and purchaser should obtain his or her own insurance.

Let's walk through the credit application and the terms and conditions, beginning with the logo, name, and address element. This is pretty basic—it clearly indicates who is extending credit and with whom the applicant is making arrangements.

Firm Name

This section provides useful information, starting with the name of the company and the contact person. The latter name is very important, because the customer is indicating who is authorized to speak for him or her concerning this account.

The address element enables you to check out the premises whenever you are suspicious, unless, of course, it is a P.O. box. In that case, secure the physical address of the business as well, which is easier to do at the outset rather than later if things don't go well.

In the event that what you are providing is resold, it is routine to request a copy of the state sales tax resale permit and federal I.D. number. Don't do business until you have these in hand.

If a purchase order is required, you have additional documentation for establishing the validity of the debt, should the account go bad. If the customer does not require one, ask for written confirmation (even a fax) of the order. This confirmation should be on his letterhead.

Principals

This section lets you know who is running the company. Certain names may be red flags.

Bank Reference

Generally speaking, you will be able to verify that they are customers in good standing. You might also be provided with average daily balances. (Note: If you want to run a periodic check on the firm, use the copy you've made of one of their payment checks and call the bank. Ask if a check for a certain amount will clear at the present time. That way, you will have some indication as to what is likely to be in their account. Remember, there's not necessarily anything wrong with their being unable to cover a check for a given amount, as the firm may be between deposits.)

Finally, the person listed as the firm's reference is usually the officer who handles their account(s). He or she may provide you with additional information, particularly if the client is a good customer. Make a note of it if they do, because you may be able to use the information somewhere down the road. Here's an example of this from my own experience.

I was performing a credit check on an applicant. Their banking reference told me that, in addition to being in good standing locally, they regularly transferred large amounts from a bank in another state. Knowing that one of the principals was from another state, I casually said the state's name with an implied question mark at the end of it. The banker confirmed that it was, indeed, that state. I made a note of it in the credit file.

A few years later the account went sour, and we had to sue. They had closed their local account and claimed to be insolvent. When we won our judgment, we had writs of garnishment served on the three banks in the out-of-state principal's hometown. Sure enough, under their corporate name there was enough money to cover what they owed us. Those assets had never been listed on their credit application, and we would not have known about them if their local banker had not, while trying to be helpful, let some valuable information slip out. If possible, get banking and other references over the phone. A chatty person will tell you things they would never put down on paper! As they say, "get it in writing." But it never hurts to "phone first"—or as a followup.

Trade (Business) References

Checking references for other businesses from which your potential client or customer purchases products or services will help verify that your credit applicant is a legitimate business. You also can learn the applicant's payment history with other suppliers. (More about these references beginning on page 38.)

Default Clause

This clause, which appears above the signature element, sets the tone for the future if they fail to pay you as agreed.

Signature Element

This element provides written proof that someone from that firm, preferably an officer, has obligated them to live up to your terms and conditions. It also makes it clear when he or she signed the agreement, which may be useful if you end up in court.

Terms and Payment

For the "Terms and Conditions of Sale" form, I have simply replicated Jackson Sound's standard terms; your own may be different. If sales tax applies to your transaction and they are claiming tax exempt status, be certain that they provide you with a "Tax Exemption Certificate acceptable to the taxing authorities" before you refrain from charging them sales tax.

Finally, the provision for additional charges should the account go bad is critical!

The balance of the form is boilerplate. Your needs may vary. Once you draft your own document, pay an attorney to read it over before you print it and start using it. The lawyer's fee will be minimal in comparison to what you might end up having to write off down the road if it turns out that your terms and conditions fail to meet legal requirements.

Terms and Conditions for Consultants

More and more organizations are turning to contract labor to perform important tasks. Consultants are usually former "permanent" managers who are now working for one or more clients, including, most often, their former employer.

If you are a consultant, you need to factor in your operation's overhead (phone, fax, stationery, copying, mileage, and so on), a fair hourly rate for yourself, and a benefits package, when you determine what your hourly rate will be. Once you have come up with your rate, provide a quotation in writing.

The first letter is a standard quote for an availability retainer. Basically, you are making yourself available on an on-call basis. This does not preclude your working for other clients, but it does mean that you will drop everything else to work for the retainer client on a moment's notice.

(Your Letterhead)

(Address Element)   (Date)

Dear

Thank you for bringing me up to speed on the Rogers merger. It seems like a good fit for you, and by combining forces, you'll be in an excellent position when deregulation takes place later this year.

I would welcome the opportunity to help with the transition on an on-call basis. My retainer rate is $3,500 a month, and I have a three-month minimum.

The $3,500 will cover up to forty hours of work within a given calendar month. Any hours in excess of forty during a given month will be billed at a rate of $75.00 per hour.

The basic retainer fee is due and payable on the first calendar day of the month, and I will submit invoices for any additional hours at month's end, with the balance due and payable on the 15th of the month. I will also enclose an invoice at month's end for any out-of-pocket expenses related to this agreement, and reimbursement is also due and payable on the 15th of the month in which my invoice is received.

Additional expenses, such as out-of-town travel, are to be paid by your firm, and you can either provide me with a travel advance, or simply handle my airfare, hotels, and so on, using one of your corporate credit cards.

This would be a revolving agreement, renewable in three-month increments, unless either party provides at least thirty days' notice of termination prior to the end of the current period. Under the agreement, I am free to handle other consulting assignments, provided that I remain available to your firm at all times.

Please send me a letter of agreement that encompasses these terms and conditions, so that we can be ready to begin when the need arises.

I am looking forward to working with you in the months ahead, as this promises to be an exciting project.

Cordially,

Out-of-pocket expenses can add up quickly! When you are spending money on behalf of a client, they are, in essence, borrowing it from you. That's why it is so important to determine in advance how you will be repaid for mileage, copying, phone calls, faxes, etc.

If a prospective client doesn't want to pay you a retainer, they run the risk of having to wait for you or not getting to work with you at all. As stated in the letter on the next page, you may want to charge occasional clients a higher hourly rate than you bill a retainer client.

(Your Letterhead)

(Address Element)   (Date)

Dear

Thank you for your inquiry concerning my availability for consulting work. When my schedule permits, my hourly rate is $110.00, with a four-hour per day minimum. My terms are net thirty days, and when I submit my invoice I will also present a bill for any out-of-pocket expenses I have incurred on your behalf.

From what you told me the other day, you will have a fair amount of work for me during the next six months. That being the case, you might want to consider a retainer agreement, as it would lower the hourly rate you would pay me.

My rate for the first forty hours of work on a retainer basis is $87.50 per hour, and any additional hours during a given calendar month would be billed at $75.00 per hour. A glance at the schedule of trade shows in which you plan to exhibit during the next several months indicates to me that you could save money by having me work the booth at a number of regional shows, rather than having to fly someone else in from headquarters.

My retainer agreements last for three-month periods and renew automatically, unless either party provides at least thirty days' notice that the agreement will not be renewed. The monthly retainer would be paid on the first calendar day of the month, and I would submit an invoice at month's end for any additional hours, along with an invoice for any out-of-pocket expenses. Both invoices would be due and payable by the 15th of the month in which they are received.

In addition to paying a lower hourly rate for my services, you would know that I am available the minute you contact me. A letter of agreement from you is all it takes to get things started.

Otherwise, my hourly rates are as stated, and I will be delighted to work with you on an as-needed basis, as my schedule permits.

Cordially,

Business References

Anyone seeking credit should provide at least three trade references of firms with whom the applicant has been doing business. Take the time to check them out.

If you have any suspicions concerning a reference, drive by and eyeball the company. A few years back, a telephone reference we checked was downright glowing, but our reference checker, who knew the city well, was suspicious. A drive-by confirmed her suspicions, as the address listed for the business was a vacant lot. It turned out that the applicant, a first-class scam artist, had an associate answer her home phone as if she were the receptionist at a thriving business. She took a message and had another associate call back an hour later with the reference.

Business Reference Call Form and Letters

A form for telephone checking follows. Use it and save it. In the event that a problem arises, it may be useful to check in with these references again to see if your debtor is still in good standing with them.

Customer/Client Name: _____	
Referred To:	Name: _____
	Street Address: _____
	_____
	Mailing Address: _____
	(if different)
	_____
Phone Number: (___) _____	
Date Called: _____	
Spoke With: _____	
Comments:	

Business reference letters are another way of finding out about how a prospective client or customer handles his money. Your applicant should provide you with the names and addresses you need to send the following letter.

(Your Letterhead)

(Address Element)   (Date)

Dear

_____ has applied for an open trade account with us and has listed your firm as a business reference. Please take the time to answer the following questions.

1. How long has this firm been doing business with you? _____

2. What are the terms of their relationship with you? (please check one)

   ❑ A. Cash only

   ❑ B. Deposit with balance due paid on receipt

   ❑ C. Open line, billed monthly

   ❑ D. Other, please specify _____

3. Please describe the firm's payment history:

   _____

   _____

4. Please feel free to make any additional comments:

   _____

   _____

   _____

Name _____Title _____Date _____

Signature _____

   Thank you very much for your time. An addressed, postage-paid envelope is enclosed for your convenience.

Sincerely,

Banking Reference Letter and Call Form

Banking references may be obtained through the mail. Many institutions shy away from third party notification (i.e., discussing a customer's credit history) without receiving permission to do so from their customer. You may provide your applicant with the following form letter to send to the officer who handles his or her accounts.

(Applicant's Letterhead)

(Address Element)   (Date)

Dear

    I have applied for an open line of credit from _____, and they have requested a banking reference. Please send them a brief letter outlining the nature of my relationship with your institution.

    Tell them how long I have been banking with you, and feel free to provide the average daily balances in my accounts.

    Your letter should be addressed to:

_____

_____

_____

Thank you very much for your prompt attention to this matter.

Sincerely,

    Phone conversations tend to be more informative because you have the ability to probe a bit. This is predicated upon the ability of your applicant's personal banker to provide you with information over the phone. Again, some banks may require permission in writing from their customer before discussing confidential information with a third party. If that is the case, use the previous letter. If, on the other hand, the applicant says that you are free to call their personal banker, do so, using the following form. Be friendly, let the banker talk to you, and take notes.

Customer/Client Name: _____

Bank's Name: _____

Location: _____

Phone: (___) _____

Fax: (___) _____

Date Called: _____

Person Contacted: _____

Title: _____

How long has applicant been banking there? _____

Account Relationships: _____

_____

Average Balances: _____

Nature of Credit Lines: _____

_____

Comments:

Financial Statements and Balance Sheets

An individual who is applying for credit should be willing to provide a financial statement. This will list his or her assets and liabilities, and the difference between the two is the net worth.

Balance sheets are used by corporations to accomplish the same thing a financial statement does for an individual. Once again, this is something any firm that is applying for credit should be willing to supply.

Let's evaluate a financial statement provided by an individual.

Individual Financial Statement Checklist

The following checklist will help you to take it apart.

---

1. What is his or her stated net worth? $_____

2. Has this statement been audited independently, or is it self-prepared?_____*

3. If real property assets have been listed, have you verified them using the assessor's office/title company form? _____

4. What warning flags do the applicant's liabilities send up? (Is there a possibility that he or she has too much of a debt burden to allow additional credit to be handled responsibly?)

5. If it is possible for you to ascertain the actual value of an equity share in one or more entities listed, have you done so?

6. Do income tax returns square with stated ability to handle credit wisely?

*As a general rule, a self-prepared one will suffice, although it is always nice to have one prepared by the individual's CPA.

Corporate Financial Statement Checklist

The closer you check things out up front, the better your chances are for not getting burned. This also applies to Corporate Balance Sheets. When you are checking one of these, request an audited version from their CPA firm. The following checklist will help you to evaluate the firm's credit worthiness.

---

1. Is it an audited statement? _____

2. Does it include:

    A. A list of assets? _____

    B. A list of all liabilities? _____

    C. An income statement? _____

If any of the above are missing, request an amended, audited statement.

3. Do their long-term liabilities threaten their ability to meet their potential obligations to you?

Assessor's Office/Title Company Contact Form

Real Property Holdings listed on a financial statement should be checked out. To do this, you will need to call either a title company or an assessor's office. The information they provide should square with what is on the financial statement, particularly in terms of ownership. If they do not, it is a red flag. Use the following form when you make your call. (Note: If the account subsequently goes bad, reverify the information on the form to see if the debtor still owns it.)

Customer/Client Name: _____

Contacted (circle one)   Assessor's Office   Title Company

Location: _____

Phone: (___)_____

Contact Name: _____

Date Contacted: _____

Results:

Street Address: _____

Full Legal Description: _____

_____

_____

Comments:

Home and Business Drive-By Inspection Form

The drive-by form is used to check out the overall appearance of the creditor's home and/or business. Someone who appears good on paper may not be such a hot prospect once you go out and eyeball where he or she lives and works. For example, an individual who headed a company with an impressive name and an address that seemed to make sense, given the business he said that he was in, turned out to be a scam artist.

One look at the "business property," an empty house on a small lot in an industrial zone, enabled us to inform the client who had hired us to check this person out that credit should not be extended. In another instance, we were able to get a banking client to close a corporate checking account when we performed a drive-by and discovered that the business address, which supposedly had a large showroom, was, in fact, a storefront private P.O. box rental operation, and the "corporation" merely rented a small box.

It turned out that they were a bunch of bad check artists, and the information we uncovered saved our client from getting badly burned. We also passed the information, with some other disquieting facts we had uncovered, to the FBI, who went about shutting the interstate operation down.

In both of the above cases, something had caused our clients to become suspicious, and their gut reactions turned out to be correct. Check things out. Here is a form to help you.

Client/Customer Name: _____

Home Address: _____

_____

_____

Date of Inspection: _____

Quality of Neighborhood: _____

Condition of Property: (Describe in detail)

Motor Vehicles on Premises:

How Many? _____

Makes and Models (Include years if known, and comment on colors and condition):

Business Name and Address: _____

_____

Date of Drive-by: _____

Comments: (Include description of the neighborhood, condition of the specific business property, how busy they appear to be, etc.)

Granting Credit

Granting credit should be a straightforward process, and it will be if your terms and conditions are spelled out clearly in advance. This goes not only for prospective clients and customers, but for your own personnel (including you) as well. While there should be a certain amount of latitude to allow for exceptional circumstances, it is imperative that you have basic policies and procedures in place at all times. What follows is a basic manual. It is intended as a guide, and you may want to alter it somewhat to meet your own needs.

Credit Granting Policy and Procedures

---

1. Purpose
This document covers our policies and procedures for granting credit. It is designed to facilitate the growth of our business, because we need to add credit-worthy individuals and firms to our customer list on an ongoing basis in order to grow and prosper.

2. Treatment
Credit applicants are to be treated courteously at all times.

3. Qualifying Prospects
Our policy is to grant credit to individuals and firms whose histories indicate that they use credit wisely. It is their responsibility to provide us with sufficient documentation to enable us to make a sound business decision. It is our responsibility to review the information applicants provide to us in a thorough and timely manner, so that a decision can be made as soon as possible.

Individuals who apply for credit must provide the following:

1. A completed application.

2. Signed copies of his/her federal tax returns for the two most recent tax years.

3. A personal financial statement that lists all of his/her assets and liabilities.

4. A copy of a current (i.e., within the past 30 days) credit bureau report.

Further, if phone calls or letters to generate the release of banking or business-related information are necessary (e.g., relevant information provided by the applicant's personal banker), the applicant agrees to effect communication with the individual(s) concerned in a timely manner. (Note: No decisions will be made concerning granting credit until all requested information has been received.)

Firms applying for credit must provide the following:

1. A completed application.

2. An audited balance sheet.

As with individual applicants, firms must also be willing to help facilitate the timely flow of information from banking and business references. Again, no decisions will be made concerning granting credit until everything requested has been received.

Our policy concerning extending credit to either individuals or firms is quite simple: If their past history indicates that they handle credit wisely, we are willing to grant credit up to the amount for which our evaluation determines they are qualified. Said amount will vary depending upon their income stream, fungible assets, and short- and long-term liabilities.

4. Formal Notification

Formal notification of our decisions shall be made in writing, on corporate letterhead. Generally, the decision reached will be one of the following:

1. The full amount requested by the individual or firm has been granted.

2. We have determined that the applicant doesn't qualify for the full amount, but we are willing to extend a lesser amount of credit.

3. The application is denied. (Note: The notification should make it clear that we welcome their business on a cash basis.)

5. Increases of Existing Credit Amounts

Increases of existing credit amounts are considered on a case-by-case basis. This may require that additional information concerning credit-worthiness be provided (e.g., written evidence of pending receivables sufficient to cover the extended obligation). In cases where a client is at the outer limits of his or her existing lines, one-time increases not to exceed $500 may be made by our account representative. Any amounts in excess of $500 must be approved by the vice president of sales.

Evaluating Credit Applicants

Evaluating the information provided by an applicant is a pretty routine matter. It is the same thing that you would do for yourself if you were looking at purchasing a big-ticket item on a time payment plan. You would look at your current expenditures and factor in additional money to be set aside for emergency use. After that, you would know how much disposable income you have left, and you could quickly determine if the projected monthly payments are more than you can afford (or want) to spend.

Applicants, individuals, and firms alike also have limits on what they can afford to spend. The information they provide will tell you how they have handled credit in the past, and their assets and liabilities will give you a clear indication of how likely it is that they will be able to meet future obligations. While none of this is risk-free, if businesses only extended credit to people and organizations who "didn't need it," there would be virtually no growth. The key is to take affordable risks, extending only as much credit as you are financially and emotionally prepared to cover.

Letters for Extending or Denying Credit

Let's look at letters for extending credit. The first is to a freelance commercial artist who has qualified for a $500 line of credit at an art supply store (if you run a business that extends credit lines to individuals, a modified version of this will serve your needs).

(Your Letterhead)

(Address Element)   (Date)

Dear

   It is with great pleasure that I write to inform you that your application for a credit line has been approved. We have opened a revolving account for you with a limit of $500.

   You will be billed monthly for all outstanding balances at an annualized rate of 12%. Your monthly invoice will be sent on the last day of the month, and a minimum payment is due within 21 calendar days of the date of the invoice. We require a minimum of 3% of the unpaid balance for amounts in excess of $15.00 Balances of less than $15.00 must be paid in full. Interest charges will be waived for the month billed if you pay your entire balance in full by the due date. This grace period should prove to be extremely helpful!

   Thank you very much for choosing us as your supplier. We look forward to serving you for many years to come.

Sincerely,

P.S. I have enclosed a copy of our statement of terms and conditions.

The next sample letter goes to the vice president of manufacturing for a company that makes a variety of products. Unfortunately, they do not qualify for the full amount of credit they have requested. However, there may still be a silver lining for all concerned.

(Your Letterhead)

(Address Element)   (Date)

Dear

    Thank you very much for your recent application to purchase $50,000 worth of widgets on credit from us. After a careful evaluation of the information provided to us we have concluded that we are unable to extend credit for the full amount.

    However, you have qualified for $35,000 worth of credit, under the terms and conditions in our standard contract. A down payment of $15,000 would enable you to acquire the full amount of widgets you would need to complete your planned manufacturing run.

    I have enclosed a revised contract that reflects the terms and conditions I have outlined in this letter. When we have received a signed contract and your down payment, we will make and ship your widgets.

    I hope that we will be able to serve you for a long time to come.

Sincerely,

Enclosure

It is always good to be optimistic about the future, even when the current news is bad, as we will see in our next letter.

(Your Letterhead)

(Address Element)   (Date)

Dear

Thank you for your recent application for credit. We regret to inform you that you do not qualify for a charge account at this time.

However, we believe that our high-quality products, first-rate customer service, and competitive pricing will make it well worth your while to do business with us on a cash basis, and we look forward to serving you.

Thank you very much for thinking of us.

Sincerely,

Many small business owners and consultants have formed corporations. By doing so, they are shielded, at least to a certain extent, from various forms of liability should something business-related go wrong. So, they tend to want everything, especially credit, to be in the organization's name rather than their own.

A formal contract binding them as individually responsible should their organization default is usually difficult to obtain, and you would need to draft such an instrument under your attorney's guidance. If their situation is shaky enough to cause you to think about this scenario, I suggest that you secure enough of a deposit in cash to cover your losses should the deal go bad.

Ironically, the money might well come from one of the principals, as he or she may simply take a cash advance on a credit card, rather than trying to borrow the money from a bank. The principal will then loan the money to his or her own company. This is a dangerous thing to do, but the main thing from your standpoint is that you get the cash you need to keep your own business running, and what you provide helps his or her business succeed.

Collection: First Letter

Ironically, your first collection letter goes out with the confirmation of a customer's first order. It is designed to strengthen the personal bond between you, making it more difficult for them to stiff you. Here's how it might go.

(Your Letterhead)

(Address Element)   (Date)

Dear

Your first order shipped today, and I wanted to take this opportunity to welcome you to our family of customers.

We pride ourselves in turning out quality products at fair prices and believe that our customer-service effort is second to none. I feel confident that you will find us to be valuable members of your manufacturing team, and I look forward to a long and mutually beneficial business relationship between our companies.

Cordially yours,

Your invoices should also contain positive statements such as:

1. Thank you for your order.

2. We appreciate your business.

3. It's a pleasure to serve you.

Showing your gratitude is not only good form from a standpoint of manners, but it also makes good sense in terms of building an ongoing relationship. The majority of individuals and firms will pay their bills in a timely manner, and they deserve your thanks, because they're the reason you're in business.

The slow-pays and no-pays we will look at next are the bane of a businessperson's existence. They are the cause of problems that range from minor irritations to threatening the solvency of their creditors' businesses. It is likely that you are dealing with one or more of them now, which is why you picked up this book. Let's work together to try to turn things around.

Collection: When the Account Is Past Due

Faxes and E-Mail to the Moderately Late

If a customer has gone thirty days beyond the due date without paying you, it is tempting to send a dunning letter using electronic transmission. Don't do this! It's too easy for your message to fall into the wrong hands—someone other than the debtor—and that's what is known as third-party notification, which is illegal and unethical. It could cause you all kinds of problems.

You are better off sending collection letters through the regular mails. You must do everything you can to keep from embarrassing the debtor publicly by inadvertently informing someone else. However, if your invoices and routine reminder calls are not getting you anywhere (e.g., the debtor will not take or return your calls), consider sending some electronic quickies via fax or E-mail.

(Your Letterhead)

(Address Element)   (Date)

Dear

  I have not heard from you lately, and I would welcome the opportunity to talk with you. Please call me today. Thanks.

Sincerely,

(Your Letterhead)

(Address Element)   (Date)

Dear

  Telephone tag is no fun! I have been unable to get through to you for some time now, and I really need to talk to you. I will be available from _____ to _____ today and tomorrow, and I have left express orders to route your call right through to me.

Sincerely,

The preceding are examples of friendly, face-saving letters. If they do not work, you might try sending the next message outside of the debtor's normal business hours. Then it is waiting when he or she gets in the next morning.

(Your Letterhead)

(Address Element)   (Date)

Dear

An urgent problem has arisen concerning your order, and I need to speak with you as soon as possible. If I am not in the office when you call, my pager number is _____.

I am sending this electronically because I have been unable to get through to you on the phone.

Awaiting your call,

What you have done is up the stakes a bit, but you are still allowing them to save face. At this point, you probably want not only to get paid, but to keep the business relationship alive. By not getting personal, you are increasing your chances of attaining both goals.

This is as far as I suggest that you go with faxes and/or E-mail. It is time to turn to regular collection letters.

Letters to the Moderately Late

In the faxes and E-mail section, I used thirty days past due as the time for you to use electronic transmission in an attempt to get your money, if your invoices and routine reminder calls aren't getting you anywhere. I began the "Moderately Late" section with the electronic letters, because I wanted to calm down people whose exasperation might have caused them to dash off a stinging letter—one that might end up causing third-party notification.

I prefer using the regular mails early on, at least where domestic collections are concerned. To me, once a customer or client is more than a week past due, I have a potential problem, and I start working the account. I do not pretend for a moment that my deadlines will apply in all cases, because credit and collection policies are necessarily varied.

All creditors have their own definition of what constitutes moderately late. Large firms who extend revolving credit lines to millions of people make phone calls and send reminder letters almost immediately to someone who is past due, but the accounts are kept open, sometimes for months!

Some companies will "freeze" a credit line until the debtor catches up, and then the line will be reopened. In both cases, the companies have such large client bases that they are able to afford a certain percentage of slow payers. Besides, bringing an account current only means that the debtor has caught up with making minimum payments, which means that it will take many years to pay off the balance in full, and all the while the interest meter is ticking. You may not be able to afford to be so "generous" with the people and/or firms who owe you money.

Personally, I maintain a policy of sending past-due accounts to an attorney at the sixty-day mark. It has not happened often, because most individuals and companies pay on time or at least make arrangements to make partial payments. On the rare occasions when customers or clients have failed to pay anything at all on their account for two months, I really do not feel that I want to do business with them again, so I have no qualms about turning their accounts over to an attorney. I will tell you more about this later on.

Once someone fails to pay off his or her balance in full, make the minimum payment due, or make partial-payment arrangements with you, and he or she is more than a week past their due date, you have a problem. It's time to send a reminder letter.

(Your Letterhead)

(Address Element)   (Date)

Re: Account #_____

Dear

   This is just a reminder that your payment of $_____ has not been received by our office. If you forgot to mail us your payment, please send it today. If you have already mailed your check, please disregard this notice.
   Thank you.

Sincerely,

Or, you might want to take this approach:

(Your Letterhead)

(Address Element)   (Date)

Re: Account #_____

Ooops!

Dear

    Did you forget to send us your payment in the amount of $_____? These days, with so much going on, it is easy to let something slip. Please send us your payment today and, if it is already on its way to us, please accept our thanks.
    We appreciate your business.

Sincerely,

You might simply want to design a little form with your name, address, phone number, and logo on it. It would also include the following:

PAST DUE NOTICE

To: (Date)

Re: Account or P.O. #_____

Balance: $_____

Minimum Payment: $_____

Your account is now past due. Please send us your payment today. Thank you.

(Name, Address, Phone, Logo)

The same format lends itself well to the following approach:

WE MISS YOU!

To: (Date)

Account/P.O. #_____

Balance Due: $_____

Minimum Payment: $_____

We have not heard from you this month, and we just wanted to remind you that your account is past due. We hope to hear from you soon!

(Name, Address, Phone, Logo)

Every so often, sometimes quite by accident, other times in an attempt to establish goodwill by sending "something," you will receive a partial payment. A simple, friendly letter will suffice.

(Your Letterhead)

(Address Element)   (Date)

Account #_____

Balance Due: $_____

Minimum Payment Due: $_____

Dear

   Thank you for your partial payment of $_____, which has been applied to your account. We appreciate your business, and we are certain that sending the wrong amount was merely an oversight. For the record, your minimum monthly payment is $_____.

   Please send us your check for at least $_____ today to bring your account up to date.

   Thank you very much.

Sincerely,

Upping the Ante

Ideally, your notice or letter will yield some results. You should either receive the payment or a phone call to make payment arrangements. If, however, another week goes by without a check, or a phone call has not been forth-coming, the debtor reaches a new plateau.

If you are at the forty-five-day mark and you have not been paid, it is time to up the ante a little. After all, in another two weeks, they will be sixty days past due!

This time, we are going to write a letter and send it via Certified Mail with a Return Receipt, evidence that it was received.

(Your Letterhead)

(Address Element)   (Date)

Re: Account #_____

Balance Due: $_____

Minimum Payment: $_____

Dear

Your account is seriously past due! You have not sent us the previous month's pay-ment and, in a short time, another monthly payment will be due.

While we appreciate your business, we find your failure to communicate with us disquieting. Please be advised that we cannot consider extending additional credit to you until you have paid off your past-due balance.

Please send us your check in the amount of $_____ today, or call our office to make arrangements.

Thank you.

Sincerely,

Collection Work Card

By now, as we rapidly near the sixty-day mark, it is time to start working the account aggressively. You are off to a good start if you send a letter by certified mail (with a return receipt requested), because that indicates that you have started a file. That being the case, it is time to introduce you to the *work card*.

Prior to the advent of the personal computer, the term "box collector" was used to describe a member of a collections team. He or she would store work cards in a file box and keep going through this portfolio, making new entries as he or she went along.

Today, computers enable collectors to do the same thing, and new systems bring up account files and phone numbers automatically when it is time to follow up on a previous call. While the old box is gradually disappearing, the work card in electronic form remains.

Old system or new, human contact is what is most important in effecting collections, because good collectors using well-honed interpersonal skills can establish relationships with debtors who are willing to work something out.

Agencies and attorneys have their own versions of the work card, and you should, too, whether you are making the collection efforts yourself or having a staff member do it for you. What follows is a generic example of what you'll need.

Name: _____

Home Phone: (____) _____

Balance Due: $ _____   Work Phone: (____) _____

Address: _____

_____

_____

_____

_____

_____

_____

_____

_____

_____

_____

_____

_____

_____

_____

_____

_____

_____

_____

_____

_____

_____

_____

_____

Let's walk through a few typical entries:

> 3/15/97: Cld wk#.Sd. to cl home 2nt. 6:00 p.m.:
> cld home. PTP current on 3/30.

Thus far the collector has managed to establish contact with the debtor, who did not want to take collection calls at work. Fine. The collector called back that evening. This time the debtor was home and promised to pay the account up to date on the 30th of the month. You will note that the collector is using a personal form of abbreviation to save space; you will find that you will develop your own style as you go along.

Please make note of the fact that the collector indicated that the debtor does not want to receive collection calls at work. Honor that type of request. Otherwise, you leave yourself open to a charge of harassment. Besides, getting personal calls at work may jeopardize the debtor's job, and if he or she loses the job, he or she is even less likely to pay you!

Business-to-business collection calls, on the other hand, are OK. By the way, if anyone tells you never to call them again, it is time to place the account with an agency or an attorney.

Let's get back to our collector. Instead of sending the promised amount on the 30th, the debtor mailed a partial payment. This generated the following letter from the collector, sent via regular mail:

(Your Letterhead)

(Address Element)   (Date)

Acct #_____

Balance Due: $_____

Dear

When I spoke with you on March 15th, you said that you would bring your account current by mailing us $_____ on the 30th. Instead, you sent us a partial payment of $_____, which has been applied to your past-due balance. Please send us a check for $_____ today to bring your account up to date. If you are unable to do so, please call me.

Thank you.

Sincerely,

If a week goes by without a payment or a call, the collector will call the debtor at home again to find out what is going on.

If you are working an account yourself, keep in mind the importance of following up regularly. If you are not using a computer, you may end up keeping your card(s) in a separate "tickler" file to remind you when you need to call.

If you are using an actual card, remember to write the debtor's balance due, phone number(s), and address in pencil, and make the rest of your entries in ink.

It is important to record all information carefully, so that there are no questions when you check the form subsequently. For the most part, you will be writing quick summaries of your calls. However, it is important that you take the time to write down critical statements uttered by the people with whom you talk. Threats, promises, and "editorial comments" should all be included.

Remember, the work card will provide you with a record of formal collection activities. It will also keep you up to date concerning the debtor's whereabouts, attitudes, and contacts. This information is invaluable to investigators, agencies, and attorneys, so keep accurate records!

The three T's are even more important as the bad debt ages:

Timing
When someone is past due, get on it right away!

Tone
Friendly (at least at the outset), polite, and professional

Tenacity
Stick with it!

Collection Letters to the Seriously Late

It's difficult to come up with a one-size-fits-all definition of the term "seriously late." Large companies with steady cash flows tend to be a lot more patient than strung-out, small business owners or consultants. As a result, the big companies keep trying to collect by using letters and phone calls, and their efforts may continue for three to six months or even more before they charge off the account and pass it on to an agency or attorney.

You, on the other hand, probably cannot afford this luxury and, if this is the case, you need to move aggressively much earlier in the game. A good way to begin is by closing the account.

(Your Letterhead)

(Address Element)   (Date)

Account #_____

Balance Due: $_____

Dear

Your account is seriously past due, and your failure to contact us leaves us no choice but to close your account, effective immediately.

We are willing to work with you, but in order to do so we need to talk with you.

Please call our office today.

Thank you.

Sincerely,

You will note that the preceding letter did not include a minimum payment amount. That is so the debtor will see the full amount due and realize why you closed the account. The fact that you are willing to work with them and are requesting only that they call you should encourage them to pick up the phone.

A letter designed to get them to make partial payments is another option you might want to consider.

(Your Letterhead)

(Address Element)   (Date)

Re: Account #_____

Past Due Balance: $_____

Dear

 We were recently forced to close your account with us because you have not made any payments since _____, and you have also failed to contact our office.

 If you are experiencing financial difficulties, we can work out a payment schedule that will enable you to deal with meeting your obligations. In order to do so, however, we need to know the problems you are facing so that we can work together to resolve them.

 Please call us today.

 Thank you.

Sincerely,

 Good collectors, once they are talking with a debtor, probe to find out what is going on. Oftentimes, the loss of a job, an illness, divorce, or simply "maxing out the plastic" results in a person becoming dysfunctional when it comes to handling his or her financial obligations. He or she is embarrassed and frequently a little frightened and reluctant to discuss the problem. A good collector will often be able to draw the debtor out.

 Collectors are not allowed to play attorney by advocating bankruptcy. In fact, they have to be very circumspect when talking with debtors. However, they can suggest that debtors who have said that they are experiencing financial difficulties contact a legitimate credit counseling service. (There are a number of bogus outfits in the field, so it pays to find out who is doing worthwhile work in your area. The collection department at your bank can tell you with whom they feel comfortable.)

 Basically, the counseling service will help the debtor to work out a payment plan that will enable him or her to gradually pay off creditors. You will have a small commission deducted from the money that is earmarked for you, but it is well worth it because you will be cashing checks on a monthly basis.

 Of course, in order for this to work, you will need a cooperative debtor. If you are dealing with someone who will not communicate, send one of the following notices.

WHAT'S GOING ON?

We cannot understand why you will not take the time to bring your seriously delinquent account current or at least call us to work out arrangements to settle your debt. Ignoring invoices and phone messages will not make this obligation go away!

Call our office today!

(Phone and Address Element)   (Date)

Account #_____

Balance Due: $_____

THE INTEREST METER IS RUNNING!

Your failure to deal with your seriously past-due account is not making your steadily increasing balance go away! The terms and conditions under which you assumed this obligation allow us to charge interest on unpaid balances. So, the balance due continues to increase.

We are willing to work with you, but the first step taken has to be yours. Call us today!

(Phone and Address Element)   (Date)

Account #_____

Balance Due as of _____: $_____

WHY WON'T YOU RETURN OUR CALLS?

Ignoring your obligations does not make them go away. This is especially true with seriously past-due debts. Late fees and interest charges cause your balance due to increase and, without your cooperation, there is nothing we can do to stop this.

Our people are willing to work with you, and we would appreciate the courtesy of a return call.

(Address and Phone Element)   (Date)

Account #_____

Balance Due: $_____

The previous notices do not have to be on your letterhead. In fact, your logo and address element at the head of the notice would weaken your opening line. Each of them is fine for dealing with individuals who refuse to contact you, but in a business-to-business relationship, you should send the following letter on your regular stationery.

(Your Letterhead)

(Address Element)   (Date)

Re: Your Past-Due Account

Dear

I must confess that I am somewhat perplexed by your refusal to at least return my calls. Your surprising failure to communicate has left me no choice but to close your firm's credit line with us.

We have supplied high quality goods and services to you in a timely manner, fully living up to the terms of our agreement. In return, we expected you to meet your obligations.

Past-due accounts are charged interest at a rate of _____. This means that, as of today, your original balance of $_____ has risen to $_____, and the balance due will continue to grow.

I hope that you will give this important matter the full attention it deserves by calling me today and making arrangements to keep your part of our bargain.

Sincerely,

Charging Off an Account and Seeking a Settlement

I have refrained from saying that a given letter or notice should be sent out at a specific time (seventy-five days, ninety days). You are free to set your own deadlines based on your specific situation.

When I was in banking, we allowed our collectors a wide degree of latitude when it came to working an account. It helped that a number of us did a great deal of outside work, because our reports gave our collectors a lot of useful information. They could determine when it was best to pass an account on to an agency or attorney. This was never done hastily. Only the hardcore deadbeats were farmed out after numerous attempts to work with them had proved fruitless.

Many rival institutions were rather rigid when it came to collections. They would send letter after letter and would not even consider sending a debt out until the 180-day past-due mark had been reached.

Charged-Off Account Checklist

While I believe that you should do everything possible to collect debts on your own, thereby saving agency and attorney fees and commissions, there comes a time when you have to realize that you have gone as far as you can with a deadbeat, and it is time to charge off the account. The following checklist will help you make that determination:

Name: _____   Date: _____

Account # _____   Balance Due: _____

1. Account is now _____ days past due.

2. Review the Work Card, business and banking reference forms, the assets form, and all correspondence relating to this account.

3. Does the debtor have assets? If yes, what are they? (Summarize briefly; e.g., owns rental house)

4. Has the debtor threatened to file bankruptcy? _____

5. Has the debtor told you never to contact him/her again? _____

6. Do you feel that the time you are spending on this account could be used more productively elsewhere? _____

7. Do you recommend the agency or attorney route? _____
   Why?

8. Could this have been prevented earlier on? _____
   How?

Going through the checklist enables you to review the history of this account. In the process, you can determine whether an agency or an attorney should take it over.

In the final part of the checklist, you have the opportunity to review your firm's credit policies. This exercise enables you to identify and solve problems. This will go a long way toward eliminating future collection problems.

Final Notices

There comes a time when preoccupation with an account that has gone bad becomes counterproductive. Going on for too long is both an emotional and a financial drain, and it can be a prelude to your going under as a viable business entity. That is because it keeps you from going after new business, and landing new customers or clients is vital to small business owners and consultants.

Desperation shows, and potential customers are quick to spot someone who is preoccupied with something. Trying to collect from someone who has no intention of paying you suffuses your being with palpable negativity, and that is likely to be enough to scare someone away from working with you.

Agencies and attorneys will tell you that, despite their best efforts, they might not be able to collect anything from your debtor. That is an ethical and reality-based statement.

Let's face facts. With bankruptcy such a readily available option, one with virtually no stigma attached to it, many debtors consider it their fall-back position. This is particularly true of people running small corporations with no personal liability for their organization's debts. Pushed to the wall, they will take the corporation under. Then they will simply start a new business.

The key is to get your money before other creditors push your debtor into bankruptcy court. If you are the only one who is going after them aggressively, they may opt to pay you at least partially, to keep things going. That is why I advocate not letting things get out of hand by waiting too long.

Settlement Computation Worksheet

The partial payment I alluded to would be in the form of a settlement. Briefly, using the worksheet on the facing page, determine the amount you are willing to settle for.

Name:_____ Date: _____

Account #_____

Balance Due: $_____

Original Balance: $_____

Amount Paid Thus Far: $_____

Calculated Loss to Date: $_____

(Note: Calculate your losses by subtracting the amount paid from the original balance due. Late fees and interest charges should not be considered at this point.)

Estimated Hours Spent Working This Account: _____

Value of Time Spent: $_____

(Note: Calculate this by multiplying the hours you spent working the account by $35. This figure will cover collection time, letter generation, and mileage and phone charges. These are tangible costs. It is very difficult to estimate intangible costs, such as lost revenue from new business because of the time spent working this account.)

Estimated Weekly Costs of Continuing to Work This Account In-house: $_____.

(Note: This figure is determined by multiplying the projected number of hours spent each week [minimum: one hour] by $35. Having determined this, estimate how long it will take you to collect the full amount due as of today. Then, subtract your estimated past and future collection costs from that amount.) The net figure will provide you with the estimated return if you keep this in-house and manage to collect the full balance due: $_____. This is your settlement figure. It allows for the waiver of late fees and interest charges, and, as it will lower the balance due significantly and put an end to the whole matter, it is an incentive for the debtor to pay you.

Add the settlement figure to the amount already collected on this account to determine your net amount: $_____ if the settlement is accepted by the debtor.

Settlement Offer Letters

After you have determined the amount you are willing to settle for, send the debtor one of the settlement offer letters shown on the following page. You will have created a win-win situation, in that the debtor's balance will drop significantly, and you will get paid!

(Your Letterhead)

(Address Element)   (Date)

Account #_____

Balance Due: $_____

Dear

    We are willing to settle this debt for a lump sum payment of $_____, which we must receive not later than _____.

    When your check clears, we will send you a final statement, marked "Paid in Full."

    We are certain that, if you weigh the alternatives, which may include legal action, you will find this to be a very attractive opportunity for you to put this debt behind you.

    If we have not received your lump sum payment by the due date, the balance due will revert to the full amount, and additional late fees and/or interest charges as allowed under the terms of our original agreement will increase the amount you owe.

    We suggest that you avail yourself of this opportunity today.

Sincerely,

(Your Letterhead)

(Address Element)   (Date)

Re: Cleaning the Slate

Dear

    You have an opportunity to put your obligation to us behind you once and for all by sending us a lump sum payment of $_____ to arrive not later than _____. As your current balance due is $_____, this one-time offer represents a savings to you of $_____.

    When your check has cleared, we will send you a final statement indicating that your balance has been paid in full.

    If you fail to respond by the due date, the balance due will revert to the full amount, so we urge you to take advantage of this offer as it is in your best interests to do so.

Sincerely,

Partial Settlement Worksheet

At this point, the debtor may make a counter-offer for either a lesser amount or a payment plan. You are in the best position to weigh the value of this offer. To do this, call a collection attorney and an agency, and find out what their percentages are when they collect. In the case of the attorney, add in any fees (service of summons, court costs, etc.) you are likely to incur at the outset. Then you will be ready to fill out the following form.

Name:_____ Date: _____

Account #_____

Our Settlement Figure: $_____

Offered Settlement: $_____

Projected Collections:

Agency: $_____(This figure is determined by subtracting the agency's commission from your settlement figure.)

Attorney: $_____(This figure is determined by subtracting the attorney's commission and any upfront out-of-pocket expenses incurred by you.)

Time Estimates (in months) for Collection:

Attorney: _____

Agency: _____

Debtor (through partial settlement): _____

Decision: (check one)

1. Accept debtor's terms _____

2. Reject terms and reiterate original settlement offer _____

3. Present counteroffer _____

Partial Settlement Letters

Here are two sample letters for accepting the debtor's offer and two for rejecting it.

(Your Letterhead)

(Address Element)   (Date)

Account #_____

Balance Due: $_____

Dear

    We have received your offer to settle this account by making a lump sum payment of $_____. We are willing to accept this amount provided that we receive the money not later than _____. Otherwise, the balance due will revert to the full amount and additional charges may also apply.

    When your check clears, we will send you a final statement marked "Paid in Full."

    Thank you.

Sincerely,

(Your Letterhead)

(Address Element)   (Date)

Account #_____

Balance Due: $_____

Dear

    We are in receipt of your offer to settle this account for $_____ not later than _____. You have offered a down payment of $_____ and monthly payments of $_____ until the settlement figure is reached.

    We are willing to accept your offer, provided that you meet your proposed payment schedule. Failure to do so will result in the balance due reverting to the full amount plus any applicable interest charges and/or late fees.

    When you have met the terms of this agreement, we will send you a final statement indicating that the balance has been paid in full.

    Thank you.

Sincerely,

(Your Letterhead)

(Address Element)   (Date)

Account #_____

Balance Due: $_____

Dear

    We have received your counteroffer to our one-time lump sum payment proposal. We are unable to accept your proposed terms.

    It is our belief that the opportunity we have presented to you to satisfy this obligation is very fair, and we will hold the offer open to you until _____. If we receive your payment in the amount of $_____ by the due date, once your check clears, we will send you a final statement marked "Paid in Full."

    Failing that, once the due date has passed, the balance due will revert to the original amount.

Sincerely,

(Your Letterhead)

(Address Element)   (Date)

Account #_____

Balance Due: $_____

Dear

    Thank you for your offer to settle this account for $_____. While we are unable to agree to your proposal, we are willing to work with you.

    Our original settlement figure of $_____ remains firm. However, we are willing to set up a payment plan that will enable you to satisfy this obligation. Please send us a down payment of $_____ to arrive not later than _____. After that, we will accept monthly payments in the amount of $_____, provided that your payments reach us by the first of the month.

    If you don't accept this offer or, having accepted it, fail to keep the arrangements, the debt will revert to the original balance due, plus any applicable interest charges and late fees.

Sincerely,

Promissory Note

Your letter tells the debtor what you will do. If the debtor agrees to make time payments, have them sign a standard promissory note. You will also sign, agreeing to the settlement figure if the debtor makes the payments as promised.

I, (print full name), acknowledge that I owe (print full name) the sum of $_____. They have offered me the opportunity to settle this obligation for the sum of $_____. I accept their offer and I promise to pay $_____ down, and to pay off the balance due in monthly installments of $_____. My payments will arrive at _____'s office not later than the first of every month.

I agree that, if I fail to keep these arrangements, the balance due will revert to the original amount due, plus any additional late fees and/or interest charges applicable under the original agreement, less any payments I have made under the terms of this promissory note.

Signed,

_____ Date: _____

Witnessed by: _____

On behalf of _____ , I agree that we will accept the terms of payment as stated in this document. Further, when we have received the funds due under this agreement, we will send _____ a final statement marked "Paid in Full."

_____ Date:_____
                 (Signature)

_____
        (Printed full name and title)

Witnessed by:

Letters Charging Off an Account

If no results are forthcoming, it is time to charge off the account and send it out. Some variations on the charged-off theme follow.

(Your Letterhead)

(Address Element)   (Date)

Account #_____

Balance Due: $_____

Dear

    This is to inform you that your account has been charged off and is now in pre-legal status. That is, we are weighing our options under the law and may send this account to an attorney or take other legal actions without further notification by us to you.

Sincerely,

(Your Letterhead)

(Address Element)   (Date)

Account #_____

Balance Due: $_____

Dear

    Your account has been charged off and has been forwarded to our attorney for immediate action.

Sincerely,

(Your Letterhead)

(Address Element)   (Date)

Account #_____

Balance Due: $_____

Dear

   This is to inform you that your account has been charged off and sent to an agency for immediate action.

Sincerely,

(Your Letterhead)

(Address Element)   (Date)

Account #_____

Balance Due: $_____

Subject: Final Notice

Dear

   If you do not send us the full amount due or fail to contact this office by ____(date)____ to make acceptable payment arrangements, this account will either be turned over to a collection agency or sent out for legal action with no further communications from this office.
   Please take the time to resolve this matter today.

Sincerely,

   The last letter leaves open the small-claims court option without actually saying so, as the term "sent out for legal action" covers all possibilities.

Taking Legal Action

It is time for you to decide which way you want to go. Before you do, answer the following question: Have you breached the original agreement in any way(s) that could leave you open to being sued by the debtor? If so, you need to be straightforward about it when you discuss the account with the agency or attorney. (Note: If you are considering small-claims court, and there is a chance that you have not met the terms of the original agreement, I advise you to take either the agency or attorney route.)

If you have failed to live up to the agreement in one or more ways, you might seriously consider accepting a settlement that finalizes this deal (in writing) and move on.

Unfortunately, a fair number of small business owners and consultants conceal things from the people who are representing them, and lawsuits have led to costly countersuits, which are frequently far from frivolous. "Yes, but . . . " is something agencies and attorneys have heard from their clients after they have worked an account and discovered that the debtor may be more the sinned against than the sinner.

This book is based on the assumption that we are talking about totally legitimate debts. However, actuarially speaking, some of my readers (not you, of course!) may have failed to live up to the terms of their own agreements. Thus, if a suit is filed, the debtor may decide to take action by suing back.

Ask yourself honestly if this matter might best be solved by reaching a settlement, rather than "taking it to the max!" Approach your agency or attorney with a reasonable settlement figure and let them work it out for you.

The Agency Route

If you determine that you are going to send a charged-off account to an agency, the first step is to complete the following form letter.

(Your Letterhead)

To: (Agency Name)   (Date)

(Address Element)

Re: Account #_____ Debtor's Name:_____

Balance Due: $_____

1. We hereby transfer this account to your agency for collection.

2. We have enclosed copies of all relevant correspondence and asset and account information.

3. Your contact person at our office is: _____ Ext. _____

4. We are willing to settle this account for: $_____.

5. If you determine that legal action is necessary, please contact our office for written instructions prior to taking action.

6. Under the terms of our agreement, we understand that your percentage of any monies collected is _____%.

7. If the debtor sends any payments to this office, they will be forwarded to you immediately.

8. Any correspondence received from the debtor by this office will be forwarded to you immediately, and if the debtor telephones us, he or she will be instructed to call your office.

_____
     (Signature)

(Printed Name and Title)

What follows is typical agency boilerplate. By law, once an account has been turned over to an agency, it must send a formal notice to the debtor. In addition to making it clear that the account is now in its hands, it provides an opportunity for the debtor to dispute the debt or a portion of it.

Often, the debtor will acknowledge the original balance, but balk at paying interest and/or penalties (e.g., late fees). Your settlement figure will give the agency some latitude when it comes to negotiating.

Once the deadline for replying expires, active collection activities begin. Bringing an agency on board makes it clear to the debtor that the account has been taken out of your hands. This will relieve you of a rather significant burden in terms of time and emotional strain.

Agencies are of particular value when the debtor has skipped, as good collectors are masters at tracking people down.

Do not begrudge the agency its commissions! Anything it brings in goes directly to your bottom line, because you have already written off the balance. Remember, be flexible when it comes to settlement arrangements. It will increase the likelihood that the debtor will be willing to make a deal and start paying.

An example of an agency's first notice follows.

(Your Letterhead)

(Date)

Re:___(Creditor's Name)_____ Account #_____ Balance: $ _____

To: (Debtor's Name)

The referenced account has been referred to our agency, and we are authorized to pursue collection.

This is an attempt to collect a debt. Any information obtained will be used for that purpose. Unless you, within thirty (30) days of receiving this notice, inform us that you dispute the validity of this debt or any portion thereof, this office will assume the debt is valid.

If you notify this office, in writing, to cease contacting you at your place of employment, no further contact shall be made. If you refuse to pay the debt or wish our agency to cease further communication and you so advise our agency, in writing, we shall not communicate with you further except:

A. To advise you that we intend to invoke specified remedies permitted by law.

B. To advise you that our efforts are being terminated.

Important: Payments and inquiries should be made to this office only.

Collection agencies are licensed by the Collection Agency Board (Address Element for Board).

Payments should not be sent to the Collection Agency Board.

(Signature)

(Printed Name and Title)

Once you turn the account over to an agency, let it work on it! When there is anything to report it will contact you. And, when it collects, it is required to remit promptly.

By placing the debt with an agency you free yourself to work on other things. Do them!

Attorney Letters

The "shot across the bow" is a letter to the debtor from an attorney. It makes it clear that things have taken a new turn, and that you are going to be aggressive about this matter.

The first letter is simple. In fact, it is a variation of your Final Notice letter. Generally speaking, you will pay the attorney a flat fee for this letter, agreeing that should it fail to yield results within a reasonable period of time, the account will be placed with the attorney on a contingency fee basis.

You may have to shop around a bit to locate a lawyer who will take an account on speculation, because too many creditors have made unrealistic, time-consuming demands of their legal representatives down through the years. For example, some creditors refuse to let go of the debt emotionally. They want instant results, so they keep "checking in," wasting the attorney's time. Simply put, let your lawyer do his or her job.

Here is an example of an Attorney Letter. You might want to have it sent by certified mail so you will receive a return receipt.

(Attorney's Letterhead)

Re: (Creditor's Name)   (Date)

Account #_____

Balance Due: $_____

Dear

Please be advised that I have been consulted by the subject creditor concerning the collection of your seriously past-due balance.

I am of the opinion that, should this matter go to trial, my client stands an excellent chance of winning a judgment for the full balance, plus additional costs, which may include fees and reasonable interest.

In order to avoid incurring additional charges related to this matter, I urge you to send my client the balance in full within seven (7) days or to contact him or her within that period to make payment arrangements.

Sincerely,

There you go! The attorney's letter should at the very least prompt a phone call to you. If satisfactory arrangements are not made, including a healthy first installment, it is time to let the attorney file suit.

You will incur some small, upfront costs for filing fees and serving the summons but after that the meter stops running. Start the ball rolling by sending the following letter.

(Your Letterhead)

To: (Attorney's Name)   (Date)

(Address Element)

Re: ___(Debtor's Name)_____   Account #_____   Balance Due: $ _____

1. We hereby place this account with you for legal action.

2. We have enclosed copies of all relevant correspondence and asset and account information.

3. Your contact person at this office is _____ Ext. _____, and he/she is authorized to make decisions on our behalf.

4. We are willing to settle this account for $_____ and realize that, whether we receive the settlement figure or the full balance due (with or without penalties), your percentage of any monies collected is _____%, after our upfront costs have been repaid to us.

5. If the debtor contacts this office in writing, the correspondence will be forwarded to you immediately, as will any payments we receive.

6. If the debtor calls this office, they will be requested to call you, as you are representing us in this matter.

7. Our check in the amount of $_____ is enclosed to cover filing fees and service of summons.

(Signature)

(Printed Name and Title)

At this point, it is time for another letter from the attorney. Armed with your settlement figure, they are in a position to negotiate when (if) the debtor or his or her attorney contacts them.

(Attorney's Letterhead)

Re: (Creditor's Name)   (Date)

Account #_____

Balance Due: $_____

Dear

Please be advised that your delinquent account has been turned over to this office for immediate collection.

Demand is made for payment in full at this time. If you cannot pay this amount in full today, you must contact me within the next five (5) days and advise me of your proposed arrangements for payment.

If I do not hear from you within this period of time, being totally ignorant of your intentions regarding payment of this debt, I will file suit without further notice to you.

Please note that the credit agreement you signed with my client provides for attorney fees and costs of collection. My time and expenses are going to be billed to and collected from you, not my client.

It is certainly to your advantage to pay the balance due before it becomes necessary to file a lawsuit to enforce payment, as further delay only increases your costs. Please take this opportunity to resolve this matter by mailing your check today for the full amount due, $_____.

I have enclosed an addressed, postage-paid envelope for your convenience.

Sincerely,

cc: (Creditor)
    Enclosure

That's it! If no results are forthcoming, the attorney will sue.

Having already given your lawyer a little negotiating wiggle room by providing a settlement figure, you have nothing more to do. That also includes going to court, if it comes to that. Your main task is to get back to trying to drum up new business!

Armed with the information you provided in the debtor's file, your attorney is ready to garnishee bank accounts and/or wages and/or place a lien or two as soon as a judgment is obtained.

I suggest skipping the court date because a lot of deadbeats simply blow it off, content to let the creditor go to the trouble and expense of winning a default judgment. After all, even when you win in court, you still have to collect. Deadbeats who believe that you will never locate the assets they squirreled away are not at all concerned about collection efforts.

Ironically, creditors with big-ticket, past-due balances sitting out there tend to let debtors slide for a longer period. These creditors usually sue later rather than sooner, and in some cases, they even continue to extend credit during prolonged periods of delinquency! They pass the additional costs on to their paying customers!

If a small business owner or consultant tries this, though, they are likely to cease to be competitive because their rates will be too high. That is why it is so important to extend credit wisely. And, if an account goes bad, get on it right away!

Aggressive collection policies and practices will give you the kind of reputation you want to have, and they will lead to prompt payments.

By the way, if you are the first to sue, you stand a better chance of getting paid. This is because a judgment, no matter how small, may start a stampede of creditors. Paying you before the court date will enable the debtor to buy time with the others, and that is decidedly to your advantage.

If someone owes you money, it is likely that he or she is in hock to other businesses and individuals. Getting paid quickly is very important, and if you are not all that certain that there are sufficient assets to cover a full balance judgment, have your attorney push for a settlement.

Intransigence on your part may cause you to miss the last opportunity to collect, so be flexible. Get your money, because money owed to the other creditors is their problem!

Foreign Collection Difficulties

If someone in another country owes you money, your collection problems are greatly exacerbated due to:

1. Currency fluctuations

2. Time differences

3. Delays in the mails

4. Jurisdictional questions

5. Cultural and linguistic differences

Let's look at each of these issues:

Currency Fluctuations

Delays in receiving payment work to your disadvantage if the currency in which you are getting paid is declining in value.

Time (Real and Perceived)

How many time zones away is the person who owes you money? Even if you have a valid phone number and he or she speaks excellent English (or you are fluent in his or her language), phone calls are a costly proposition. And, if there is a language barrier, even if you are using an interpreter, the elapsed time per call can run up a huge phone bill.

The concept of time also varies from one place to another. The country your debtor is from may have a more elastic view of the passage of time, and they may be wondering why you are making such a big deal out of something that, in their culture, would not be considered late at all.

The Mails

Sending something via air mail only guarantees that your letter will leave the United States on a plane. When it arrives, it may sit in a central post office for weeks before it is sent on. While the temptation may be strong to send a dunning letter using fax or E-mail, I suggest that you send your letter(s) via an air courier service. Then you know they will arrive in a timely manner, and you avoid the danger of third-party notification.

Jurisdiction

If you do have to sue, you will need to establish where the suit must be filed. If it is in the debtor's country (or even another state in the United States, for that matter), you have a major problem. You will need to hire an attorney in that venue, and you are going to have to pay him an upfront retainer and various other fees. Even if you can go to trial in your own town, the debtor still needs to be served, and he or she may be overseas where having a summons served can be a costly proposition and difficult to verify.

Cultural and Linguistic Differences

We have already looked at the concept of time, which may be very different in the debtor's country. Extrapolating from that, we need to understand that delaying payment may impart additional status to the debtor, because it enables the debtor to be in control of the business relationship. Let's look at a real-life example:

A businessman I know is dealing with a foreign business entity, one that could easily afford to pay him in what we in the United States would consider to be a timely manner. Instead, they initially played a game with him, paying him for his consulting services months after they had been invoiced.

He understands their culture, and he did not press them for payment. This gave him status in their eyes because he did not appear to need the money. At the same time, once he completed a project and invoiced them, he politely refused to do anything else until they brought themselves current. He made it clear that he was not in a hurry to get paid, but his policies were firm with regard to taking on new work.

As they really needed him, they began paying within two weeks of receiving his invoices, and they have maintained that schedule ever since. (Even when they were dragging things out, he still did OK, as he had other clients who paid promptly, and with his foreign clients he ups his hourly rate to include "interest.")

Let's turn now to language. Americans think English, in comparison to many other languages, is rather simple and direct. It is often called the language of international business, although Japanese and various forms of Chinese are beginning to stake their own claims to that title. Many businesspeople around the world speak and read English, but truly understanding it is another matter, and communications problems, even under the best of circumstances, frequently arise.

Translations are one way of dealing with this, although some things simply do not translate readily into another language, and the concept of "face" (i.e., respect for the dignity of the individual) also comes into play. Whether you are writing in English or sending a translation, real and staged communications problems can plague you because your letter is imprecise and/or you have gravely offended its recipient. Like it or not, we have to keep these things in mind when we are doing business in the international marketplace.

Granting Credit to Foreign Firms

You can nip a lot of potential problems in the bud by doing everything you can to get paid early on. While it is exciting and flattering to be approached by a foreign firm (or to have one respond favorably to your overtures), don't be blinded by the glamour of it all! Pay strict attention to vital details from the outset.

International Credit Checklist

Here is a handy form to help you keep track of information concerning potential foreign customers.

Name: _____ Date: _____

U.S. Representative: _____ Phone: (___) _____

Firm Name: _____ Fax: (___) _____

Address: _____

Referred By: _____ Phone: (___) _____

Type of Business: _____

Proposed Nature of Our Relationship: _____

_____

_____

Credit Application Sent To: _____ Date: _____
Name and Title

Completed Application Received On: _____

Referrals are quite common in business, and it is useful to note who has referred prospective clients and customers to you. You should follow up with a thank-you phone call and, whenever possible, reciprocate.

On the other hand, if you made the contact yourself at a trade show or convention, jot down the name and the date of the gathering. Likewise, if their U.S. representative approached you, note that.

International Credit Letters

Your first letter should accompany the credit application. The following example is addressed to a firm's U.S. representative.

(Your Letterhead)

(Address Element)   (Date)

Re: (Name of Foreign Firm/Individual)

Dear

    Thank you very much for your time the other day. I enjoyed meeting with you, and I welcome the opportunity to serve as your client's U.S. distributor. I have enclosed our standard credit application. Please complete it and send it back to me at your earliest convenience.

Cordially,

    Regardless of how big the client, you need to get an agreement in writing before you extend credit. You also need to check references prior to writing the following letter.

(Your Letterhead)

(Address Element)   (Date)

Re: (Name of Foreign Firm/Individual)

Dear

    I am delighted to inform you that we are ready to begin serving as _____'s U.S. distributor. Please feel free to contact me at any time should questions arise.
    Looking forward to a long and mutually profitable relationship, I remain, yours truly,

---

    Send a copy to the individual who provided the initial referral, and write a large "Thank You!" on the letter.
    Thus far, we have only dealt with U.S.-based representatives, and we have confined ourselves to English. In some cases, you may need to write to someone at the company itself and, if you do so, there are two options:

1. Send a standard letter in English.

2. Draft a letter in English and have a certified translator rewrite it in your intended recipient's language. Send the latter letter, keeping your original English version and a copy of the translated letter for your files.

The firm's representative will indicate which path you need to take. You should also address the issue of what language(s) your formal agreement should be in. Make sure that your attorney has gone over it thoroughly before you sign it and send it out.

The vast majority of us, even if we are fluent in another language, are incapable of drafting a contract in that language. The services of an attorney and a translator are critical. Agreements, which may end up being reviewed in court, frequently contain legal terms, and you are better off spending the money to hire competent legal and linguistic help up front rather than inadvertently providing loopholes that might let a debtor get away.

Even seemingly routine correspondence can be tricky, and you need to know the cultural and linguistic nuances that can make all the difference. If you don't know them, use the services of someone who does.

Foreign Collections

Contacting the Moderately Late

If you are dealing with someone outside of the United States, phone calls can be quite costly and mail may take a long time to arrive. While I counsel against the use of electronic transmission for dunning letters, there is no harm in sending a friendly fax that does not allude to the debt. Translated versions may be necessary in all forms of correspondence. Here are two examples in English:

(Your Letterhead)

(Address Element)   (Date)

Dear

    I would welcome the opportunity to speak with you at your earliest convenience. Given the time differences between our countries, calling me at my normal business hours may be difficult for you. If that is the case, your call would be most welcome outside of U.S. business hours. My home number is _____.

    I look forward to hearing from you soon.

Sincerely,

(Your Letterhead)

(Address Element)   (Date)

Dear

    I have not heard from you for some time, and I am quite concerned. I would welcome the opportunity to speak with you at any time, day or night. If calling me at my office during normal U.S. business hours is not convenient for you, you may also reach me at my home _____.

    I hope that all is well, and I look forward to hearing from you soon.

Sincerely,

    Some people don't like the idea of giving out their home phone number, and they don't like taking business calls during the evening or on weekends. However, many small business owners and consultants who do business internationally are on the phone day and night, even when the news is good. If someone in another country owes you a significant amount of money, you are probably going to be awake most of the time anyway.

    If you are dealing with a foreign firm's U.S. representative, the standard collection letters to the moderately late we looked at earlier will suffice and, for that matter, so will the domestic fax and E-mail variations. As any good collector will tell you, the first step is to get the debtor on the phone. While that is fine for domestic collections, phone calls to foreign-based firms and individuals can cost you a fortune, not to mention lead to misunderstandings (real and feigned) if there is a language barrier. So letters are the way to go, using an air courier service if necessary. Here are several letters to the moderately late.

(Your Letterhead)

(Address Element)   (Date)

Dear

    The mails can be slow, and we are certain that your payment is on its way to us. If it is, please disregard this reminder.

    We greatly value our business relationship and hope to continue serving you. In order to do so, timely payments are a must, as our domestic suppliers bill us promptly for the goods and services that they provide to us.

    We look forward to receiving your payment soon. A copy of our invoice is enclosed for your records.

Cordially,

(Your Letterhead)

(Address Element)   (Date)

Dear

    We have yet to receive your payment of the enclosed invoice. Hopefully, your check is on its way to us at the present time and has simply been delayed in the mails. If not, please send it to us upon receipt of this reminder so that we may continue to serve you. Thank you very much.

Sincerely,

(Your Letterhead)

(Address Element)   (Date)

Dear

    I am writing to inform you that we have yet to receive payment for _____ (a copy of the original invoice is enclosed). As a result, we are regrettably forced to suspend the extension of further credit at this time.

    If your payment is not already on its way to us, please arrange for a wire transfer to our bank (_____) upon receipt of this letter, so that we may resume serving you.

    Thank you very much.

Sincerely,

What If They Are Seriously Late?

Now you really have a problem. It is time to do some serious thinking. Here are your options:

1. Do nothing. Let the balance due simply sit there on your books and hope that the debtor will pay you if and when they discover they still need you.

2. Continue to mail them invoices, adding interest and late fees to the balance due (if your agreement allows), hoping all the while that they will send you the money some day.

3. Place the account with an agency.

4. See if an attorney is willing to take this on a contingency fee basis. It is unlikely that you will find one who will, so you need to decide how much you are willing to pay a lawyer to tackle this. Jurisdiction can be a problem, and you may need to hire an attorney in the debtor's country, which can increase your costs enormously.

5. Sell the debt for cents on the dollar, and put the whole thing behind you. This is becoming an increasingly popular option, as it pays the creditor something right away and the purchaser incurs all future expenses. The amount has to be big enough to interest an agency or syndicate so that it will make you an offer, but it is worth looking into.

    Let's weigh the pros and cons of the proactive options I've mentioned.

Agency
Pro—No up-front money from you. *Con*—They are likely to confine themselves to sending letters. Agency's percentage: _____

Attorney (Domestic, Contingency Fee Basis)
Pro—No up-front money except for filing fees and service of summons (if you can sue them locally). *Con*—Debtor's assets may be overseas. Attorney's percentage: _____

Attorney (Domestic, Fee Basis)
Pro—If they are really good you may have a chance. *Con*—You are paying them from the get-go. Key issue—How much do they estimate this will cost?

Attorney (Foreign, Fee Basis)
Pro—If jurisdiction is a problem, they are right where you need them. *Con*—You cannot monitor their work, and the meter is always running. Key issue—What are your chances of winning in a foreign court against a local national?

Buyout
Pro—You will get some money, right away. *Con*—That is all you will ever get.

Letter Advising Possible Legal Action

While you are weighing the alternatives, send the following letter via air courier:

(Your Letterhead)

(Address Element)   (Date)

Re: Past Due Balance of $_____

Final Notice

Dear

    I regret to inform you that your account has been placed on prelegal status. Thus we are examining all of our options under the law to effect collection of this debt. These may include placing the account with an agency, selling the debt to a third party, or filing a lawsuit. Any of these actions may incur additional charges to you.

    As in the past, we remain willing to work with you, and we will accept a lump sum payment of $_____ in U.S. funds as full settlement of this debt, provided the amount is wire transferred to our bank, _____, Account# _____, not later than _____.

    If this deadline is not met, the balance due will revert to the full amount (plus any additional charges allowed under the terms of our original agreement), and we will avail ourselves of one of the options available to us under the law.

    This is the final communication you will receive from this office.

Sincerely,

    While you are waiting for their reply, do some comparison shopping over the course of a week or two. Interview attorneys and agencies. Also inquire if anyone is buying foreign debt.

    Call your local office of the National Association of Credit Management, and ask for referrals to its members who buy or collect foreign debt. If there is no office in your area, call the national headquarters (1-800-955-8815).

    When you have weighed your options, take action.

Summary

The next time around, arrange for your foreign client to pay you with a letter of credit. These are rather complicated things, but a banker with international experience can explain how they work and prepare them for you.

    Prior to talking with a banker, I suggest that you read Chapter 9 in Czinkota, Ronkainen, and Tarrant's *The Global Marketing Imperative* (1995: NTC).

    Well-constructed credit agreements can lead to rewarding relationships; the kinds that benefit both parties.

Global trade barriers are falling and, as former U.S. Commerce Secretary Mickey Kantor told me in an interview, "The big firms have been trading internationally for years. Now small businesses and consultants can get in the game!" Good luck!

As you see, a letter written with no resolve behind it is not enough to get the job done. It is imperative that you be aggressive when it comes to attempting to effect collections. This is because, in an age when so many people readily avail themselves of the protection afforded by bankruptcy, those who make serious collection efforts early on will actually collect.

In other aspects of our lives, we have no qualms about seeking help when we need it. We rely on physicians, mechanics, plumbers, etc., to do things for us. While their bills do not thrill us, we realize that they do something of value for us and what we pay them is money well spent. If you need to call in a collections professional to put some teeth behind your letters, then do it. Your business's health is worth it.

As in medicine, prevention is better than attempting to cure when running a business. I hope that by using the guidelines in this book, you will refine your credit policies so that you will be able to prevent most collection problems from happening in the first place.

It is important to enter business relationships with two types of capital: financial and emotional. Then you will be able to weather the storms and make your business grow.

Timing . . . tone . . . tenacity—Put the three T's to work for you today!

Part III

The Credit and Collection Kit of Letters and Forms

Credit Application

Firm name:_____ Contact person: _____

Address: _____

City:_____ State: _____ ZIP: _____

Kind of business: _____ In business since:_____

Telephone: _____ Resale number: _____

State sales tax resale #: _____ (Attach copy) Federal I.D.: _____

Purchase order required? Yes:_____ No: _____

Corporation: _____ Partnership:_____ Sole owner: _____

Principals: President: _____ _____

Vice pres.: _____ _____

Secretary: _____

Bank Reference

Name: _____ Acct. #:_____

Address: _____

City:_____ State: _____ ZIP: _____

Telephone: _____

Contact: _____ Banked here since: _____

Trade References

Firm name:_____ Telephone: _____

Address: _____

Contact: _____

Firm name:_____ Telephone: _____

Address: _____

Contact: _____

Firm name:_____ Telephone: _____

Address: _____

Contact: _____

The undersigned hereby agrees that should a credit account be opened, and in the event of default in the payment of any amount due, and if such account is submitted to a collection authority, to pay an additional charge equal to the cost of collection including court costs.

Applicant company_____ Date _____

Signature _____ Title _____

Full name of signator (please print) _____

Terms and Conditions of Sale

1. Terms and Payment

(a) Terms of payment are 50% deposit with order, with balance due at time of delivery. Arrangements for credit must be made in advance. Purchaser agrees to submit its most current financial information and bank and trade references, if requested.

(b) All sales, use excise, or similar tax applicable to sales pursuant to this agreement shall be paid by the purchaser, unless purchaser provides seller with a Tax Exemption Certificate acceptable to the taxing authorities.

(c) In the event that the purchase account becomes overdue or delinquent, seller shall be entitled to reimbursement from purchaser for seller's reasonable expenses of collection, including attorney fees. Seller may charge the lesser of 1.5% per month or the highest lawful monthly contract rate on overdue accounts.

2. Price, Shipment, and Delivery Terms

(a) Due to the uncertainty of costs, prices are subject to change without notice.

(b) All deliveries are F.O.B. seller's facility.

3. Warranty: Limitation of Liability

(a) Seller warrants to the original purchaser that the product will be free from defects in material and workmanship for a period of 30 days from date of delivery. Seller's sole liability (and purchaser's only remedy) for any defect shall be to replace or repair, at seller's option, any materials which seller reasonably determines to have a defect covered by its warranty within a reasonable time, and without charge.

(b) Except for the repair/replacement described in this paragraph, seller shall not be liable for damages of any kind arising out of either the use of the material furnished hereunder or its failure to function properly.

(c) Material which has been subject to alteration, misuse, misapplication, negligence or action shall be excluded from warranty coverage.

The above warranty is in lieu of any other warranty, whether express, implied, or statutory including but not limited to any warranty of merchantability fitness for any particular purpose, freedom from infringement, or the like, and any warranty otherwise arising out of any proposal, specification, or sample. Seller neither assumes nor authorizes any person to assume for it any other liability.

4. Exclusion of Damages

In no event shall seller be liable for any consequential, incidental, indirect, exemplary, or special damages, whether in contract or in tort, in any action, in connection with this agreement or the material furnished hereunder.

5. Rights, Licenses, Copyrights, and Indemnification

(a) Purchaser shall secure all rights, licenses, and copyrights for anything to be recorded, produced, or duplicated in any way by seller. Purchaser warrants that it is the legal owner or licensee for purposes of duplication for any material supplied to seller, and seller shall be held harmless by purchaser from any and all claims by third parties.

(b) Purchaser shall indemnify and hold seller harmless from all suits, claims, demands, and other clauses of action and expenses arising out of or in connection with the production, duplication, or distribution of products, materials, or services that seller shall have furnished.

6. General

(a) The interpretation and performance of this agreement are governed by the laws of the State of _____.

(b) It is agreed that sales are made on the terms, conditions, and warranties contained herein. To the extent of any conflict, these terms and conditions take precedence over any on purchaser's order form. No agreement shall be valid unless in writing, duly signed by the parties.

7. Merchandise Return

Seller must be notified within 30 days from the date of delivery or pickup or purchaser's order of any problem, defect, miscount, or other reason for the return of any merchandise ordered.

8. Customer Property

(Seller's corporate name) is not responsible for any loss or damage of/to materials or master tapes stored or used. (Seller's corporate name)'s insurance does not cover this and purchaser should obtain his or her own insurance.

Terms and Conditions for Consultants

(Your Letterhead)

(Address Element)   (Date)

Dear

    Thank you for bringing me up to speed on the Rogers merger. It seems like a good fit for you, and by combining forces, you'll be in an excellent position when deregulation takes place later this year.

    I would welcome the opportunity to help with the transition on an on-call basis. My retainer rate is $3,500 a month, and I have a three-month minimum.

    The $3,500 will cover up to forty hours of work within a given calendar month. Any hours in excess of forty during a given month will be billed at a rate of $75.00 per hour.

    The basic retainer fee is due and payable on the first calendar day of the month, and I will submit invoices for any additional hours at month's end, with the balance due and payable on the 15th of the month. I will also enclose an invoice at month's end for any out-of-pocket expenses related to this agreement, and reimbursement is also due and payable on the 15th of the month in which my invoice is received.

    Additional expenses, such as out-of-town travel, are to be paid by your firm, and you can either provide me with a travel advance, or simply handle my airfare, hotels, and so on, using one of your corporate credit cards.

    This would be a revolving agreement, renewable in three-month increments, unless either party provides at least thirty days' notice of termination prior to the end of the current period. Under the agreement, I am free to handle other consulting assignments, provided that I remain available to your firm at all times.

    Please send me a letter of agreement that encompasses these terms and conditions, so that we can be ready to begin when the need arises.

    I am looking forward to working with you in the months ahead, as this promises to be an exciting project.

Cordially,

(Your Letterhead)

(Address Element)   (Date)

Dear

Thank you for your inquiry concerning my availability for consulting work. When my schedule permits, my hourly rate is $110.00, with a four-hour per day minimum. My terms are net thirty days, and when I submit my invoice I will also present a bill for any out-of-pocket expenses I have incurred on your behalf.

From what you told me the other day, you will have a fair amount of work for me during the next six months. That being the case, you might want to consider a retainer agreement, as it would lower the hourly rate you would be paying me.

My rate for the first forty hours of work on a retainer basis is $87.50 per hour, and any additional hours during a given calendar month would be billed at $75.00 per hour. A glance at the schedule of trade shows in which you plan to exhibit during the next several months indicates to me that you could save money by having me work the booth at a number of regional shows, rather than having to fly someone else in from headquarters.

My retainer agreements last for three-month periods and renew automatically, unless either party provides at least thirty days' notice that the agreement will not be renewed. The monthly retainer would be paid on the first calendar day of the month, and I would submit an invoice at month's end for any additional hours, along with an invoice for any out-of-pocket expenses. Both invoices would be due and payable by the 15th of the month in which they are received.

In addition to paying a lower hourly rate for my services, you would know that I am available the minute you contact me. A letter of agreement from you is all it takes to get things started.

Otherwise, my hourly rates are as stated, and I will be delighted to work with you on an as-needed basis, as my schedule permits.

Cordially,

Business Reference Call Form and Letter

Customer/Client Name: _____

Referred To: Name: _____

                   Street Address: _____

                   _____

                   Mailing Address: _____
                   (if different)

                   _____

Phone Number: (___) _____

Date Called: _____

Spoke With: _____

Comments:

(Your Letterhead)

(Address Element)   (Date)

Dear

_____ has applied for an open trade account with us and has listed your firm as a business reference. Please take the time to answer the following questions.

1. How long has this firm been doing business with you? _____

2. What are the terms of their relationship with you?
   (please check one)

   ❏ A. Cash only

   ❏ B. Deposit with balance due paid on receipt

   ❏ C. Open line, billed monthly

   ❏ D. Other, please specify _____

3. Please describe the firm's payment history:

   _____

   _____

4. Please feel free to make any additional comments:

   _____

   _____

   _____

Name_____ Title_____ Date _____

Signature _____

   Thank you very much for your time. An addressed, postage-paid envelope is enclosed for your convenience.

Sincerely,

Banking Reference Letter

(Applicant's Letterhead)

(Address Element)   (Date)

Dear

    I have applied for an open line of credit from _____, and they have requested a banking reference. Please send them a brief letter outlining the nature of my relationship with your institution.

    Tell them how long I have been banking with you, and feel free to provide the average daily balances in my accounts.

    Your letter should be addressed to:

_____

_____

_____

Thank you very much for your prompt attention to this matter.

Sincerely,

Banking Reference Call Form

Customer/Client Name: _____

Bank's Name: _____

Location: _____

Phone: (___) _____

Fax: (___) _____

Date Called: _____

Person Contacted: _____

Title: _____

How long has applicant been banking there? _____

Account Relationships: _____

_____

Average Balances: _____

Nature of Credit Lines: _____

_____

Comments:

Individual Financial Statement Checklist

1. What is his or her stated net worth? $_____

2. Has this statement been audited independently, or is it self-prepared?_____*

3. If real property assets have been listed, have you verified them using the assessor's office/title company form? _____

4. What warning flags do the applicant's liabilities send up? (Is there a possibility that he or she has too much of a debt burden to allow additional credit to be handled responsibly?)

5. If it is possible for you to ascertain the actual value of an equity shares in one or more entities listed, have you done so?

6. Do income tax returns square with stated ability to handle credit wisely?

*As a general rule, a self-prepared one will suffice, although it is always nice to have one prepared by his or her CPA.

Corporate Financial Statement Checklist

1. Is it an audited statement? _____

2. Does it include:

    A. A list of assets? _____

    B. A list of all liabilities? _____

    C. An income statement? _____

If any of the above are missing, request an amended, audited statement.

3. Do their long-term liabilities threaten their ability to meet their potential obligations to you?

Assessor's Office/Title Company Contact Form

Customer/Client Name: _____

Contacted (circle one)   Assessor's Office   Title Company

Location: _____

Phone: (____) _____

Contact Name: _____

Date Contacted: _____

Results:

Street Address: _____

Full Legal Description: _____

_____

_____

Comments:

Home and Business Drive-By Inspection Form

Client/Customer Name: _____

Home Address: _____

_____

_____

Date of Inspection: _____

Quality of Neighborhood: _____

Condition of Property: (Describe in detail)

Motor Vehicles on Premises:

How Many? _____

Makes and Models (Include years if known, and comment on colors and condition):

Business Name and Address: _____

_____

Date of Drive-by: _____

Comments: (Include description of the neighborhood, condition of the specific business property, how busy they appear to be, etc.)

Credit Granting Policy and Procedures

1. Purpose
This document covers our policies and procedures for granting credit. It is designed to facilitate the growth of our business, because we need to add credit-worthy individuals and firms to our customer list on an ongoing basis in order to grow and prosper.

2. Treatment
Credit applicants are to be treated courteously at all times.

3. Qualifying Prospects
Our policy is to grant credit to individuals and firms whose histories indicate that they use credit wisely. It is their responsibility to provide us with sufficient documentation to enable us to make a sound business decision. It is our responsibility to review the information applicants provide to us in a thorough and timely manner, so that a decision can be made as soon as possible.

Individuals who apply for credit must provide the following:

1. A completed application.

2. Signed copies of his/her tax returns for the two most recent tax years.

3. A personal financial statement that lists all of his/her assets and liabilities.

4. A copy of a current (i.e., within the past 30 days) credit bureau report.

Further, if phone calls or letters to generate the release of banking or business-related information are necessary (e.g., relevant information provided by the applicant's personal banker), the applicant agrees to effect communication with the individual(s) concerned in a timely manner. (Note: No decisions will be made concerning granting credit until all requested information has been received.)

Firms applying for credit must provide the following:

1. A completed application.

2. An audited balance sheet.

As with individual applicants, firms must also be willing to help facilitate the timely flow of information from banking and business references. Again, no decisions will be made concerning granting credit until everything requested has been received.

Our policy concerning extending credit to either individuals or firms is quite simple: If their past history indicates that they handle credit wisely, we are willing to grant credit up to the amount for which our evaluation determines they are qualified. Said amount will vary depending upon their income stream, fungible assets, and short- and long-term liabilities.

(Continued on next page)

4. Formal Notification

Formal notification of our decisions shall be made in writing, on corporate letterhead. Generally, the decision reached will be one of the following:

1. The full amount requested by the individual or firm has been granted.

2. We have determined that the applicant doesn't qualify for the full amount, but we are willing to extend a lesser amount of credit.

3. The application is denied. (Note: The notification should make it clear that we welcome their business on a cash basis.)

5. Increases of Existing Credit Amounts

Increases of existing credit amounts are considered on a case-by-case basis. This may require that additional information concerning credit-worthiness be provided (e.g., written evidence of pending receivables sufficient to cover the extended obligation). In cases where a client is at the outer limits of their existing lines, one-time increases not to exceed $500 may be made by our account representative. Any amounts in excess of $500 must be approved by the vice president of sales.

Letters for Extending or Denying Credit

(Your Letterhead)

(Address Element)   (Date)

Dear

It is with great pleasure that I write to inform you that your application for a credit line has been approved. We have opened a revolving account for you with a limit of $500.

You will be billed monthly for all outstanding balances at an annualized rate of 12%. Your monthly invoice will be sent on the last day of the month, and a minimum payment is due within 21 calendar days of the date of the invoice. We require a minimum of 3% of the unpaid balance for amounts in excess of $15.00 Balances of less than $15.00 must be paid in full. Interest charges will be waived for the month billed if you pay your entire balance in full by the due date. This grace period should prove to be extremely helpful!

Thank you very much for choosing us as your supplier. We look forward to serving you for many years to come.

Sincerely,

P.S. I have enclosed a copy of our statement of terms and conditions.

(Your Letterhead)

(Address Element)   (Date)

Dear

Thank you very much for your recent application to purchase $50,000 worth of widgets on credit from us. After a careful evaluation of the information provided to us we have concluded that we are unable to extend credit for the full amount.

However, you have qualified for $35,000 worth of credit, under the terms and conditions in our standard contract. A down payment of $15,000 would enable you to acquire the full amount of widgets you would need to complete your planned manufacturing run.

I have enclosed a revised contract that reflects the terms and conditions I have outlined in this letter. When we have received a signed contract and your down payment, we will make and ship your widgets.

I hope that we will be able to serve you for a long time to come.

Sincerely,

Enclosure

(Your Letterhead)

(Address Element)   (Date)

Dear

    Thank you for your recent application for credit. We regret to inform you that you do not qualify for a charge account at this time.

    However, we believe that our high-quality products, first-rate customer service, and competitive pricing will make it well worth your while to do business with us on a cash basis, and we look forward to serving you.

    Thank you very much for thinking of us.

Sincerely,

Collection: First Letter

(Your Letterhead)

(Address Element)   (Date)

Dear

    Your first order shipped today, and I wanted to take this opportunity to welcome you to our family of customers.

    We pride ourselves in turning out quality products at fair prices and believe that our customer-service effort is second to none. I feel confident that you will find us to be valuable members of your manufacturing team, and I look forward to a long and mutually beneficial business relationship between our companies.

Cordially yours,

Faxes and E-Mail to the Moderately Late

(Your Letterhead)

(Address Element)   (Date)

Dear

    I have not heard from you lately, and I would welcome the opportunity to talk with you. Please call me today. Thanks.

Sincerely,

(Your Letterhead)

(Address Element)   (Date)

Dear

    Telephone tag is no fun! I have been unable to get through to you for some time now, and I really need to talk to you. I will be available from _____ to _____ today and tomorrow, and I have left express orders to route your call right through to me.

Sincerely,

(Your Letterhead)

(Address Element)   (Date)

Dear

An urgent problem has arisen concerning your order, and I need to speak with you as soon as possible. If I am not in the office when you call, my pager number is _____.

I am sending this electronically because I have been unable to get through to you on the phone.

Awaiting your call,

Letters to the Moderately Late

(Your Letterhead)

(Address Element)   (Date)

Re: Account #_____

Dear

This is just a reminder that your payment of $_____ has not been received by our office. If you forgot to mail us your payment, please send it today. If you have already mailed your check, please disregard this notice.

Thank you.

Sincerely,

(Your Letterhead)

(Address Element)   (Date)

Re: Account #_____

Ooops!

Dear

     Did you forget to send us your payment in the amount of $_____? These days, with so much going on, it is easy to let something slip. Please send us your payment today and, if it is already on its way to us, please accept our thanks.
     We appreciate your business.

Sincerely,

PAST DUE NOTICE

To:

Re: Account or P.O. #_____

Balance: $_____

Minimum Payment: $_____

Your account is now past due. Please send us your payment today. Thank you.

(Name, Address, Phone, Logo)

WE MISS YOU!

To: (Date)

Account/P.O. #_____

Balance Due: $_____

Minimum Payment: $_____

We have not heard from you this month, and we just wanted to remind you that your account is past due. We hope to hear from you soon!

(Name, Address, Phone, Logo)

(Your Letterhead)

(Address Element)   (Date)

Account #_____

Balance Due: $_____

Minimum Payment Due: $_____

Dear

Thank you for your partial payment of $_____, which has been applied to your account. We appreciate your business, and we are certain that sending the wrong amount was merely an oversight. For the record, your minimum monthly payment is $_____.

Please send us your check for at least $_____ today to bring your account up to date.

Thank you very much.

Sincerely,

Upping the Ante

(Your Letterhead)

(Address Element)   (Date)

Re: Account #_____

Balance Due: $_____

Minimum Payment: $_____

Dear

    Your account is seriously past due! You have not sent us the previous month's payment and, in a short time, another monthly payment will be due.

    While we appreciate your business, we find your failure to communicate with us disquieting. Please be advised that we cannot consider extending additional credit to you until you have paid off your past-due balance.

    Please send us your check in the amount of $_____ today, or call our office to make arrangements.

    Thank you.

Sincerely,

Collection Work Card

Name: _____

Home Phone: (___) _____

Balance Due: $ _____   Work Phone: (___) _____

Address: _____

_____

_____

_____

_____

_____

_____

_____

_____

_____

_____

_____

_____

_____

_____

_____

_____

_____

_____

_____

_____

_____

_____

_____

Response to Partial Payment

(Your Letterhead)

(Address Element)   (Date)

Acct #_____

Balance Due: $_____

Dear

    When I spoke with you on March 15th, you said that you would bring your account current by mailing us $_____ on the 30th. Instead, you sent us a partial payment of $_____, which has been applied to your past-due balance. Please send us a check for $_____ today to bring your account up to date. If you are unable to do so, please call me.
    Thank you.

Sincerely,

Collection Letters to the Seriously Late

(Your Letterhead)

(Address Element)   (Date)

Account #_____

Balance Due: $_____

Dear

    Your account is seriously past due, and your failure to contact us leaves us no choice but to close your account, effective immediately.
    We are willing to work with you, but in order to do so we need to talk with you.
    Please call our office today.
    Thank you.

Sincerely,

(Your Letterhead)

(Address Element)   (Date)

Re: Account #_____

Past Due Balance: $_____

Dear

    We were recently forced to close your account with us because you have not made any payments since _____, and you have also failed to contact our office.

    If you are experiencing financial difficulties, we can work out a payment schedule that will enable you to deal with meeting your obligations. In order to do so, however, we need to know the problems you are facing so that we can work together to resolve them.

    Please call us today.

    Thank you.

Sincerely,

WHAT'S GOING ON?

We cannot understand why you will not take the time to bring your seriously delinquent account current or at least call us to work out arrangements to settle your debt. Ignoring invoices and phone messages will not make this obligation go away!

    Call our office today!

(Phone and Address Element)   (Date)

Account #_____

Balance Due: $_____

THE INTEREST METER IS RUNNING!

Your failure to deal with your seriously past-due account is not making your steadily increasing balance go away! The terms and conditions under which you assumed this obligation allow us to charge interest on unpaid balances. So, the balance due continues to increase.

We are willing to work with you, but the first step taken has to be yours. Call us today!

(Phone and Address Element)   (Date)

Account #_____

Balance Due as of _____: $_____

WHY WON'T YOU RETURN OUR CALLS?

Ignoring your obligations does not make them go away. This is especially true with seriously past-due debts. Late fees and interest charges cause your balance due to increase and, without your cooperation, there is nothing we can do to stop this.

Our people are willing to work with you, and we would appreciate the courtesy of a return call.

(Address and Phone Element)   (Date)

Account #_____

Balance Due: $_____

(Your Letterhead)

(Address Element)   (Date)

Re: Your Past-Due Account

Dear

I must confess that I am somewhat perplexed by your refusal to at least return my calls. Your surprising failure to communicate has left me no choice but to close your firm's credit line with us.

We have supplied high quality goods and services to you in a timely manner, fully living up to the terms of our agreement. In return, we expected you to meet your obligations.

Past-due accounts are charged interest at a rate of _____. This means that, as of today, your original balance of $_____ has risen to $_____, and the balance due will continue to grow.

I hope that you will give this important matter the full attention it deserves by calling me today and making arrangements to keep your part of our bargain.

Sincerely,

Charged-Off Account Checklist

Name: _____   Date: _____

Account # _____   Balance Due: _____

1. Account is now _____ days past due.

2. Review the Work Card, business and banking reference forms, the assets form, and all correspondence relating to this account.

3. Does the debtor have assets? If yes, what are they? (Summarize briefly, e.g., owns rental house)

4. Has the debtor threatened to file bankruptcy? _____

5. Has the debtor told you never to contact him/her again? _____

6. Do you feel that the time you are spending on this account could be used more productively elsewhere? _____

7. Do you recommend the agency or attorney route? _____
   Why?

8. Could this have been prevented earlier on? _____
   How?

Settlement Computation Worksheet

Name:_____   Date: _____

Account #_____

Balance Due: $_____

Original Balance: $_____

Amount Paid Thus Far: $_____

Calculated Loss to Date: $_____

(Note: Calculate your losses by subtracting the amount paid from the original balance due. Late fees and interest charges should not be considered at this point.)

Estimated Hours Spent Working This Account: _____

Value of Time Spent: $_____

(Note: Calculate this by multiplying the hours you spent working the account by $35. This figure will cover collection time, letter generation, and mileage and phone charges. These are tangible costs. It is very difficult to estimate intangible costs, such as lost revenue from new business because of the time spent working this account.)

Estimated Weekly Costs of Continuing to Work This Account In-house: $_____.

(Note: This figure is determined by multiplying the projected number of hours spent each week [minimum: one hour] by $35. Having determined this, estimate how long it will take you to collect the full amount due as of today. Then, subtract your estimated past and future collection costs from that amount.) The net figure will provide you with the estimated return if you keep this in-house and manage to collect the full balance due: $_____. This is your settlement figure. It allows for the waiver of late fees and interest charges, and, as it will lower the balance due significantly and put an end to the whole matter, it is an incentive for the debtor to pay you.

Add the settlement figure to the amount already collected on this account to determine your net amount: $_____ if the settlement is accepted by the debtor.

Settlement Offer Letters

(Your Letterhead)

(Address Element)   (Date)

Account #_____

Balance Due: $_____

Dear

   We are willing to settle this debt for a lump sum payment of $_____, which we must receive not later than _____.

   When your check clears, we will send you a final statement, marked "Paid in Full."

   We are certain that, if you weigh the alternatives, which may include legal action, you will find this to be a very attractive opportunity for you to put this debt behind you.

   If we have not received your lump sum payment by the due date, the balance due will revert to the full amount, and additional late fees and/or interest charges as allowed under the terms of our original agreement will increase the amount you owe.

   We suggest that you avail yourself of this opportunity today.

Sincerely,

(Your Letterhead)

(Address Element)   (Date)

Re: Cleaning the Slate

Dear

You have an opportunity to put your obligation to us behind you once and for all by sending us a lump sum payment of $_____ to arrive not later than _____. As your current balance due is $_____, this one-time offer represents a savings to you of $_____.

When your check has cleared, we will send you a final statement indicating that your balance has been paid in full.

If you fail to respond by the due date, the balance due will revert to the full amount, so we urge you to take advantage of this offer as it is in you best interests to do so.

Sincerely,

Partial Settlement Worksheet

Name:_____   Date: _____

Account #_____

Our Settlement Figure: $_____

Offered Settlement: $_____

Projected Collections:

Agency: $_____(This figure is determined by subtracting the agency's commission from your settlement figure.)

Attorney: $_____(This figure is determined by subtracting the attorney's commission and any upfront out-of-pocket expenses incurred by you.)

Time Estimates (in months) for Collection:

Attorney: _____

Agency: _____

Debtor (through partial settlement): _____

Decision: (check one)

1. Accept debtor's terms _____

2. Reject terms and reiterate original settlement offer _____

3. Present counteroffer _____

Partial Settlement Letters

(Your Letterhead)

(Address Element)   (Date)

Account #_____

Balance Due: $_____

Dear

    We have received your offer to settle this account by making a lump sum payment of $_____. We are willing to accept this amount provided that we receive the money not later than _____. Otherwise, the balance due will revert to the full amount and additional charges may also apply.

    When your check clears, we will send you a final statement marked "Paid in Full."

    Thank you.

Sincerely,

(Your Letterhead)

(Address Element)   (Date)

Account #_____

Balance Due: $_____

Dear

We are in receipt of your offer to settle this account for $_____ not later than
_____. You have offered a down payment of $_____ and monthly payments
of $_____ until the settlement figure is reached.

We are willing to accept your offer, provided that you meet your proposed payment schedule. Failure to do so will result in the balance due reverting to the full
amount plus any applicable interest charges and/or late fees.

When you have met the terms of this agreement, we will send you a final statement indicating that the balance has been paid in full.

Thank you.

Sincerely,

(Your Letterhead)

(Address Element)   (Date)

Account #_____

Balance Due: $_____

Dear

    We have received your counteroffer to our one-time lump sum payment proposal. We are unable to accept your proposed terms.

    It is our belief that the opportunity we have presented to you to satisfy this obligation is very fair, and we will hold the offer open to you until _____. If we receive your payment in the amount of $_____ by the due date, once your check clears, we will send you a final statement marked "Paid in Full."

    Failing that, once the due date has passed, the balance due will revert to the original amount.

Sincerely,

(Your Letterhead)

(Address Element)   (Date)

Account #_____

Balance Due: $_____

Dear

    Thank you for your offer to settle this account for $_____. While we are unable to agree to your proposal, we are willing to work with you.

    Our original settlement figure of $_____ remains firm. However, we are willing to set up a payment plan that will enable you to satisfy this obligation. Please send us a down payment of $_____ to arrive not later than _____. After that, we will accept monthly payments in the amount of $_____, provided that your payments reach us by the first of the month.

    If you don't accept this offer or, having accepted it, fail to keep the arrangements, the debt will revert to the original balance due, plus any applicable interest charges and late fees.

Sincerely,

Promissory Note

I, (print full name), acknowledge that I owe (print full name) the sum of $_____. They have offered me the opportunity to settle this obligation for the sum of $_____. I accept their offer and I promise to pay $_____ down, and to pay off the balance due in monthly installments of $_____. My payments will arrive at _____'s office not later than the first of every month.

I agree that, if I fail to keep these arrangements, the balance due will revert to the original amount due, plus any additional late fees and/or interest charges applicable under the original agreement, less any payments I have made under the terms of this promissory note.

Signed,

_____ Date: _____

Witnessed by: _____

On behalf of _____ , I agree that we will accept the terms of payment as stated in this document. Further, when we have received the funds due under this agreement, we will send _____ a final statement marked "Paid in Full."

_____ Date: _____
(Signature)

_____
(Printed full name and title)

Witnessed by:

Letters Charging Off an Account

(Your Letterhead)

(Address Element)   (Date)

Account #_____

Balance Due: $_____

Dear

    This is to inform you that your account has been charged off and is now in pre-legal status. That is, we are weighing our options under the law and may send this account to an attorney or take other legal actions without further notification by us to you.

Sincerely,

(Your Letterhead)

(Address Element)   (Date)

Account #_____

Balance Due: $_____

Dear

    Your account has been charged off and has been forwarded to our attorney for immediate action.

Sincerely,

(Your Letterhead)

(Address Element)   (Date)

Account #_____

Balance Due: $_____

Dear

    This is to inform you that your account has been charged off and sent to an agency for immediate action.

Sincerely,

(Your Letterhead)

(Address Element)   (Date)

Account #_____

Balance Due: $_____

Subject: Final Notice

Dear

    If you do not send us the full amount due or fail to contact this office by ____(date)____ to make acceptable payment arrangements, this account will either be turned over to a collection agency or sent out for legal action with no further communications from this office.

    Please take the time to resolve this matter today.

Sincerely,

The Agency Route Letters

(Your Letterhead)

To: (Agency Name)   (Date)

(Address Element)

Re: Account #: _____ Debtor's Name: _____

Balance Due: $_____

1. We hereby transfer this account to your agency for collection.

2. We have enclosed copies of all relevant correspondence and asset and account information.

3. Your contact person at our office is: _____ Ext. _____

4. We are willing to settle this account for: $_____.

5. If you determine that legal action is necessary, please contact our office for written instructions prior to taking action.

6. Under the terms of our agreement, we understand that your percentage of any monies collected is _____%.

7. If the debtor sends any payments to this office, they will be forwarded to you immediately.

8. Any correspondence received from the debtor by this office will be forwarded to you immediately, and if the debtor telephones us, he or she will be instructed to call your office.

_____ (Signature)

(Printed Name and Title)

(Your Letterhead)

(Date)

Re:___(Creditor's Name)_____ Account #_____ Balance: $ _____

To: (Debtor's Name)

The referenced account has been referred to our agency, and we are authorized to pursue collection.

This is an attempt to collect a debt. Any information obtained will be used for that purpose. Unless you, within thirty (30) days of receiving this notice, inform us that you dispute the validity of this debt or any portion thereof, this office will assume the debt is valid.

If you notify this office, in writing, to cease contacting you at your place of employment, no further contact shall be made. If you refuse to pay the debt or wish our agency to cease further communication and you so advise our agency, in writing, we shall not communicate with you further except:

A. To advise you that we intend to invoke specified remedies permitted by law.

B. To advise you that our efforts are being terminated.

Important: Payments and inquiries should be made to this office only.

Collection agencies are licensed by the Collection Agency Board (Address Element for Board).

Payments should not be sent to the Collection Agency Board.

(Signature)

(Printed Name and Title)

Attorney Letters

(Attorney's Letterhead)

Re: (Creditor's Name)   (Date)

Account #_____

Balance Due: $_____

Dear

   Please be advised that I have been consulted by the subject creditor concerning the collection of your seriously past-due balance.

   I am of the opinion that, should this matter go to trial, my client stands an excellent chance of winning a judgment for the full balance, plus additional costs, which may include fees and reasonable interest.

   In order to avoid incurring additional charges related to this matter, I urge you to send my client the balance in full within seven (7) days or to contact him or her within that period to make payment arrangements.

Sincerely,

(Your Letterhead)

To: (Attorney's Name)   (Date)

(Address Element)

Re: ___(Debtor's Name)_____ Account #_____ Balance Due: $ _____

1. We hereby place this account with you for legal action.

2. We have enclosed copies of all relevant correspondence and asset and account information.

3. Your contact person at this office is _____ Ext. _____, and he/she is authorized to make decisions on our behalf.

4. We are willing to settle this account for $_____ and realize that, whether we receive the settlement figure or the full balance due (with or without penalties), your percentage of any monies collected is _____%, after our upfront costs have been repaid to us.

5. If the debtor contacts this office in writing, the correspondence will be forwarded to you immediately, as will any payments we receive.

6. If the debtor calls this office, they will be requested to call you, as you are representing us in this matter.

7. Our check in the amount of $_____ is enclosed to cover filing fees and service of summons.

(Signature)

(Printed Name and Title)

(Attorney's Letterhead)

Re: (Creditor's Name)   (Date)

Account #_____

Balance Due: $_____

Dear

Please be advised that your delinquent account has been turned over to this office for immediate collection.

Demand is made for payment in full at this time. If you cannot pay this amount in full today, you must contact me within the next five (5) days and advise me of your proposed arrangements for payment.

If I do not hear from you within this period of time, being totally ignorant of your intentions regarding payment of this debt, I will file suit without further notice to you.

Please note that the credit agreement you signed with my client provides for attorney fees and costs of collection. My time and expenses are going to be billed to and collected from you, not my client.

It is certainly to your advantage to pay the balance due before it becomes necessary to file a lawsuit to enforce payment, as further delay only increases your costs. Please take this opportunity to resolve this matter by mailing your check today for the full amount due, $_____.

I have enclosed an addressed, postage-paid envelope for your convenience.

Sincerely,

cc: Creditor
    Enclosure

International Credit Checklist

Name: _____ Date: _____

U.S. Representative: _____ Phone: (___)_____

Firm Name: _____ Fax: (___)_____

Address: _____

Referred By: _____ Phone: (___)_____

Type of Business: _____

Proposed Nature of Our Relationship: _____

_____

_____

Credit Application Sent To: _____ Date: _____
Name and Title

Completed Application Received On: _____

International Credit Letters

(Your Letterhead)

(Address Element)   (Date)

Re: (Name of Foreign Firm/Individual)

Dear

　　Thank you very much for your time the other day. I enjoyed meeting with you, and I welcome the opportunity to serve as your client's U.S. distributor. I have enclosed our standard credit application. Please complete it and send it back to me at your earliest convenience.

Cordially,

(Your Letterhead)

(Address Element)   (Date)

Re: (Name of Foreign Firm/Individual)

Dear

    I am delighted to inform you that we are ready to begin serving as _____'s U.S. distributor. Please feel free to contact me at any time should questions arise.

    Looking forward to a long and mutually profitable relationship, I remain, yours truly,

Foreign Collection Letters

(Your Letterhead)

(Address Element)   (Date)

Dear

    I would welcome the opportunity to speak with you at your earliest convenience. Given the time differences between our countries, calling me at my normal business hours may be difficult for you. If that is the case, your call would be most welcome outside of U.S. business hours. My home number is _____.

    I look forward to hearing from you soon.

Sincerely,

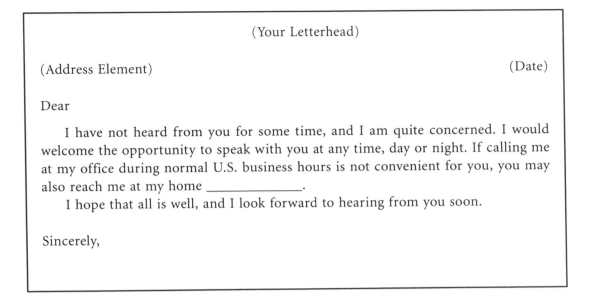

(Your Letterhead)

(Address Element)   (Date)

Dear

    I have not heard from you for some time, and I am quite concerned. I would welcome the opportunity to speak with you at any time, day or night. If calling me at my office during normal U.S. business hours is not convenient for you, you may also reach me at my home _____.

    I hope that all is well, and I look forward to hearing from you soon.

Sincerely,

(Your Letterhead)

(Address Element)   (Date)

Dear

    The mails can be slow, and we are certain that your payment is on its way to us. If it is, please disregard this reminder.

    We greatly value our business relationship and hope to continue serving you. In order to do so, timely payments are a must, as our domestic suppliers bill us promptly for the goods and services that they provide to us.

    We look forward to receiving your payment soon. A copy of our invoice is enclosed for your records.

Cordially,

(Your Letterhead)

(Address Element)   (Date)

Dear

   We have yet to receive your payment of the enclosed invoice. Hopefully, your check is on its way to us at the present time and has simply been delayed in the mails. If not, please send it to us upon receipt of this reminder so that we may continue to serve you. Thank you very much.

Sincerely,

(Your Letterhead)

(Address Element)   (Date)

Dear

   I am writing to inform you that we have yet to receive payment for _____ (a copy of the original invoice is enclosed). As a result, we are regrettably forced to suspend the extension of further credit at this time.
   If your payment is not already on its way to us, please arrange for a wire transfer to our bank (_____) upon receipt of this letter, so that we may resume serving you.
   Thank you very much.

Sincerely,

Letter Advising Possible Legal Action

(Your Letterhead)

(Address Element)   (Date)

Re: Past Due Balance of $_____

Final Notice

Dear

    I regret to inform you that your account has been placed on prelegal status. Thus we are examining all of our options under the law to effect collection of this debt. These may include placing the account with an agency, selling the debt to a third party, or filing a lawsuit. Any of these actions may incur additional charges to you.

    As in the past, we remain willing to work with you, and we will accept a lump sum payment of $_____ in U.S. funds as full settlement of this debt, provided the amount is wire transferred to our bank _____, Account# _____, not later than _____.

    If this deadline is not met, the balance due will revert to the full amount (plus any additional charges allowed under the terms of our original agreement), and we will avail ourselves of one of the options available to us under the law.

    This is the final communication you will receive from this office.

Sincerely,

Appendix

Ethics

The National Association of Credit Management's (NACM) Canons of Business Credit Ethics are worth reading. They are reprinted here with permission.

1. Justice, equity and confidence constitute the foundation of credit administration.

2. Agreements and contracts reflect integrity and should never be breached by either party.

3. The interchange of credit information must be based upon confidence, cooperation, reciprocity and confidentiality.

4. It is deemed unethical to be a party to unwarranted assignments or transfers of an insolvent debtor's assets, nor should creditors participate in secret arrangements.

5. Creditors should cooperate for the benefit of all in adjustment or liquidation of insolvent estates or companies.

6. Creditors must render all possible assistance to honest debtors who become insolvent.

7. Dishonest debtors must be exposed and referred to the authorities.

8. Cooperation, fairness and honesty must dominate in all insolvent debtor proceedings.

9. Costly administrative procedures in the rehabilitation or liquidation of an insolvent debtor shall be avoided at all times.

10. Members pledge themselves to uphold the integrity, dignity and honor of the credit professional in all of their business dealings.

There would be very little business if no credit was extended, so the world needs credit and collections professionals. Properly practiced, theirs is an honorable pursuit, and I urge you to deal with ethical professionals at all times.

The NACM provides a wide range of services to its members, including business credit reports, business collections, industry credit groups, distressed business services, and educational programs. They also have numerous publications that are reasonably priced and available to members and nonmembers alike.

The group is expanding its worldwide credit information network, which may be helpful to you if you're doing business internationally.

They have offices in many U.S. cities, so check the business section of your phone book or call (800) 955-8815. Their headquarters address is:

National Association of Credit Management
8815 Centre Park Drive, Suite 200
Columbia, MD 21045-2117
Phone: (410) 740-5560
Fax: (410) 740-5574

They may be able to help you do a better job, and it doesn't hurt to check them out.

About the Author

Ed Halloran teaches marketing and management courses at Columbia College's Extended Studies Center in Aurora, Colorado. He also runs a multimedia production company in Denver.

Ed worked in credit and collections at a large financial institution for a number of years and subsequently co-founded an agency that conducts asset searches and effects collections for a variety of clients. The agency's success led to the initial funding of the production company.

Ed's experiences as an "outside man" (i.e., field investigator) and his many contacts in business, law enforcement, and the legal profession enable him to provide the reader with a wide variety of collection techniques.